CRIME IN TEXAS

K E N   A N D E R S O N

CRIME IN TEXAS

Your Complete Guide to the Criminal Justice System

REVISED EDITION

UNIVERSITY OF TEXAS PRESS, *Austin*

Printed in the United States of America
Revised edition, 2005

♾ The paper used in this publication meets the minimum requirements of American National Standard for Information Sciences—Permanence of Paper for Printed Library Materials, ANSI Z39.48-1984.

Library of Congress Cataloging-in-Publication Data have been requested.

TO NELL MYERS,
the founder of People Against Violent Crime,
whose courage and determination have inspired so many of us,

&

TO THE CHILDREN,
yours and mine,
who deserve the safest possible Texas that we can make.

Note to the Reader: Every effort has been made to ensure the accuracy of the information in this book. However, the reader should be aware that at any time a court decision, the legislative process, or a change in administrative policy can affect information contained herein.

CONTENTS

CRIME IN TEXAS

INTRODUCTION

Kenneth McDuff. More than any other person, McDuff has come to represent everything that was wrong with the Texas criminal justice system. He convinced everyone—citizens, politicians, the news media—just how truly broken the Texas system was.

The facts of his case are worth repeating. If we are to avoid the mistakes of the past, we must remember the awful lesson McDuff inflicted on Texas.

Kenneth McDuff was a dangerous, cold-blooded killer. He was a dangerous, cold-blooded killer the August 1966 night that he murdered three Fort Worth teenagers. He was a dangerous, cold-blooded killer when the parole board voted to release him in October 1989. He was a dangerous, cold-blooded killer those days in 1991 and 1992 when he killed Melissa Northrup and Colleen Reed. And he remained a dangerous, cold-blooded killer until his execution on November 17, 1998.

McDuff was born and raised in Texas. Although he had several incidents with school and law enforcement officials, he managed to stay out of prison until age 19. In 1965, he was convicted of a string of 12 burglaries and received a 4-year prison sentence. After less than one year, he was paroled—given a second chance.

McDuff responded to this second chance by going on a vicious murder rampage in Tarrant County. On the night of August 6, 1966, McDuff and a buddy selected at random, then robbed and abducted, three teenagers. McDuff forced them into a car trunk. Later, as the boys begged him to spare their lives, he shot them in the head a total of five times. McDuff and his buddy repeatedly raped the girl. McDuff then killed her by choking her with a broomstick.

McDuff was tried, convicted, and sentenced to death. He spent six years on death row before the 1972 United States Supreme Court decision ruling that all current death penalty laws, including Texas', were unconstitutional. (A new, constitutional death penalty law was put into effect in 1974.) McDuff and Texas' other 87 death row inmates had their sentences commuted to life. Under the parole law at that time, he became eligible for release in 1976. He was repeatedly denied parole. Out of desperation, he offered a $10,000 bribe to a parole official. In 1982, he was convicted of the bribery attempt, but the jury gave him only a 2-year sentence.

Meanwhile, Texas politicians continued to pass tough anticrime laws but neglected to build the prison space needed to back up the laws. As prison crowding became a severe problem, a federal judge ruled that the crowding was unconstitutional and took control of the Texas prison system. State officials tried to buy time and space by increasing good-time credits, releasing more inmates on parole, and paroling tens of thousands of inmates before they even reached prison. At the system's worst, inmates served 22 days for each year of their sentences; parole approval rates skyrocketed to 80%.

Of those released early, many committed more crimes and reentered the system. This, in turn, pushed other inmates out early, who then committed more crimes. The process was repeated in a sickeningly futile cycle.

In October 1989, as the system melted down, it did the unthinkable and released Kenneth McDuff. His record showed 16 felony convictions, 12 burglaries, and 3 murders, as well as his 1982 bribery conviction.

McDuff didn't stay out of trouble for long. By July 1990, he was arrested for the misdemeanor offense of making a terroristic threat. Parole violation charges put McDuff safely back behind bars.

Then the unthinkable occurred again.

Falls County officials dropped their charges. Why? Their witnesses were reluctant to testify, saying they hoped that the parole board would, nonetheless, use McDuff's criminal conduct to revoke his parole and keep him in prison. The board, still paroling prisoners far too early, made an administrative decision. The board did not seek a revocation based on the terroristic threat and simply released McDuff. On December 6, 1990, at the end of the year when the parole rate peaked, McDuff was free again.

We don't know the exact details of the next seventeen months. McDuff's crime spree included drug dealing, robberies, and possibly nine murders. For certain, we know that on December 30, 1991, he kidnapped Colleen Reed from an Austin car wash. He raped, brutalized, and finally murdered her. Then on March 1, 1992, McDuff kidnapped and killed Melissa Northrup, a 22-year-old Waco convenience store worker. That spring, McDuff became the object of a massive manhunt. Finally, after being featured on *America's Most Wanted* TV show, McDuff was discovered working as a trash collector in Kansas City, Missouri. On May 4, 1992, he was arrested.

McDuff was tried, convicted, and sentenced to death for the murders of Reed and Northrup. He spent six years on death row until his execution on November 17, 1998.

Why are McDuff's victims dead? Under any rational prison system, no matter how overcrowded or understaffed, McDuff would have been recognized as a vicious killer who should never have been released. The system utterly failed in its primary function—to protect its citizens.

Although hundreds of other dangerous criminals released early also committed heinous crimes, the McDuff debacle galvanized public opinion like no other case. The Texas Legislature passed sweeping reforms, and citizens overwhelmingly voted for a billion-dollar bond to finance more prison beds. The result was dramatic:

- The prison system expanded from 38,000 beds to 140,000 beds.
- Good time was significantly reformed.
- Minimum parole eligibility doubled for violent offenders.
- The pace of executions picked up, and Texas executed more killers than any other state.

Had all these reforms been in effect in 1966, Kenneth McDuff's case would have turned out differently. He probably would have been executed a very long time ago. If he'd somehow been able to avoid execution, his life sentence for capital murder would have required him to serve 40 calendar years rather than 10 before the parole board would have even considered him. When his time came, he would not have been considered by a three-member panel of the board, as in the typical case. The full 18-member parole board would have reviewed his case. He would have needed 12 votes. Before they could vote, the board would have had to have listened to any presentation the victims' loved ones wanted to make.

The bottom line: under the laws enacted in the wake of the McDuff case, he either would have been executed years ago or still be at least a year away from an initial parole review on the 1966 Tarrant County murders. He would have found this initial review heavily stacked against him. Far more important, Colleen Reed, Melissa Northrup, and perhaps seven other women would still be alive today.

For the past twenty-nine years, I have been involved with the criminal justice system. I have lived and worked in a prison unit. I did a two-year stint as a research assistant with Texas' highest criminal court, the Court of Criminal Appeals, and for the past twenty-five years I have served Williamson County as an assistant district attorney, district attorney, and in my current position of state district judge.

During that time I have talked to far too many relatives of murder victims, held the hands of far too many young victims of child abuse, investigated far too many tragedies brought on by alcohol and drug abuse. I have also heard far too many politicians who talk about getting tough on crime but who are not willing to pay for prison beds. I have seen far too much news coverage of the trivial and obvious that failed to explain the big picture. Frankly, if politicians had backed up their rhetoric with funding, and if the news media had been more aggressive in their coverage, the flood of early releases and the system meltdown that led to McDuff's release might not have occurred.

I wrote this book so that every Texan can understand our system and our laws. We need to have such an understanding to intelligently cast our ballots and influence our local and state government to provide effective law enforcement. Such an understanding is our best hope for avoiding future Kenneth McDuffs.

Before beginning a step-by-step explanation of the Texas legal system, I will start by briefly discussing four current trends that help to explain much of what is happening behind today's newspaper headlines:

- Reforms inspired by the breakdown in the system
- Declining crime rate
- Prevention/enforcement combinations that work
- Recognition of victims' rights

REFORMS Just as the McDuff case dramatically illustrates how broken the system was, so the reforms it spawned show how forcefully the public responded. Across the state, laws and policies became a lot tougher. The parole board immediately stopped paroling bad risks. The parole approval rate, which hovered near 80% in 1991, declined to 50% in 1992 and then to barely 20% by 1994. The parole board kept the approval rate in the mid-20% range through 2003. The post-McDuff years brought dozens of other changes—some small, some huge—that increased the amount of time inmates, particularly violent inmates, had to serve. These changes

- doubled to 30 calendar years the minimum parole eligibility for a violent offender doing life
- increased to 40 calendar years the minimum parole eligibility for a capital killer who is not executed
- expanded the definition of a violent crime to include all child molesters
- overhauled the good-time system to ensure that it is used only as a reward for truly good behavior
- vastly increased the punishments for drunk drivers who kill or seriously injure others
- abolished Texas' formerly very liberal prison furlough program whereby inmates could be released, unguarded, for up to a week for any "appropriate reason," including visits to relatives and friends

These very significant changes became real when Texas embarked on the largest prison construction program in the world. A system that had once held just 38,000 prisoners was expanded to 140,000 by 1997 and has since grown to hold 152,000. In addition, the system added thousands of juvenile beds and community corrections beds. Local jails were enlarged until the jail system, which houses misdemeanants and felons awaiting trial, now can hold more than 78,000 inmates.

The Texas prison system, the largest in the United States, is now the world's third largest—behind only China and Russia. Texas also has the toughest laws in the nation for violent criminals—as well as the prison beds to back up those laws. On any given night, Texas law enforcement officers can lock up 230,000 criminals.

As a result, the crime rate has gone down. It has gone down dramatically.

DECLINING CRIME RATE These reforms may have cost a lot of money, but we have been receiving the benefits. Folk wisdom assures us that taxes and crime are two things that will never go down. Well, Texas is now showing the nation the contrary. Crime can be brought down.

Texas began using its current system for tracking its reported crime rate in 1976. Such a rate—the number of crimes per 100,000 citizens—automatically controls for population increases. The crime rate in Texas increased steadily after 1976. But the number of prison beds didn't. The largest crime increases came in the mid- to late-1980s, when early release from prisons freed tens of thousands of inmates.

These unabated crime-rate increases finally turned around in 1992. The very spring that Kenneth McDuff captured headlines around the nation, parole rates declined and other reforms began. The Texas crime rate declined 9.7% in 1992, 8.8% in 1993, and another 8.8% in 1994. The total decline from 1991 to 1995 was a whopping 27.3%. These reductions correspond directly to reductions in the parole rate —from 80% in 1991 to barely 20% in 1995. Common sense tells us that the crime rate declined because more criminals were in prison.

But would it last? Could tougher punishments, fewer paroles, and more prison beds not only lower the crime rate, but keep it low? The answer to both questions was a resounding Yes! The most dramatic decline was in the murder rate, which fell 58% between 1991 and 2003. But all the index crimes showed huge drops: rape, down 32%; robbery, down 42%; aggravated assault, down 29%; burglary, down 45%; theft, down 25%, and car theft, down 53%. The overall crime rate declined an incredible 34% between 1991 and 2003.

Let's put it another way. Texas had 312,719 burglaries in 1991. In the next twelve years, the burglary rate declined an incredible 45%. Because it did, during those twelve years, 1,216,242 Texas families who otherwise would have been victims got up in the morning and went to work or school. When they returned home, everything was in its place. No one had pried open the door, ransacked the house, or taken the jewelry, deer rifle, and VCR. These Texans don't know who they are and will never be the subject of a TV newscast, but their lives are better because the system was fixed.

The legislature that met in the spring of 1993 considered the recommendation of a statewide group, the Punishment Standards Commission. Made up of members of the legislature and many judges, but no prosecutors, the commission wanted to respond to prison crowding by significantly lowering punishments. For example, they recommended lowering the maximum punishment for nearly all violent offenses from life to 20 years and allowing for automatic release after criminals had served 80% of their time. In effect, they wanted to lower punishments so that the maximum sentences would be the same as the then-early release sentences. Punishments for other offenses would be even lower. House burglary, which had carried a possible life sentence, was to carry a maximum of 4 years.

I was part of a group locked in a heated battle with supporters of the Punishment Standards Commission. My group favored building more prisons and increasing punishments. One spring day, I testified in front of the Senate committee, chaired by Senator John Whitmire, that was considering these reforms. To no one's surprise, I was urging that we build prison beds and increase punishments. I told the senators that the parole board could not indefinitely lower parole rates without tens of thousands of new prison beds.

Then I made a promise. If they adopted the new laws and built the beds, the crime rate in Texas would decline dramatically.

The room became very quiet. No one had ever made such a statement. I heard a few snickers and then some whispers that I should never have promised a lower crime rate.

I know about the dangers of promising too much. The Texas crime rate had gone up, with only minor pauses, for some fifteen straight years. But I was absolutely convinced that crime had gone up because of early releases and that eliminating them would bring the crime rate down.

Dr. Tony Fabelo, head of the now defunct Texas Criminal Justice Policy Council, was among those in the audience that day who were skeptical that we could either achieve or maintain a significant crime-rate reduction. It is obvious that we have achieved and maintained such a reduction; the reduction has now lasted for more than a decade. While I have a tremendous respect for Dr. Fabelo and other skeptical professionals, all Texans can be glad that the skeptics were wrong.

Meanwhile, newspaper headlines will continue to report crime statistics in terms of one-year "trends." When crime next fluctuates upward, which it must inevitably do, the headline will shout, "Crime Soars." But unless the news media relate any increases to 1991 figures, they will be presenting a terribly misleading picture to Texas citizens. The next time you read a crime-rate story in the newspaper, judge for yourself whether the media puts the rate in a long-term context: do they relate it to 1991 figures, or do they simply relate it to last year's figures?

PREVENTION/ENFORCEMENT COMBINATIONS THAT WORK In 1980, Candy Lightner was a California mother. When a drunk driver killed her daughter, Candy was told, "It's just one of those things." The killer would never serve a day in jail, they said.

Within two years, Candy Lightner had founded Mothers Against Drunk Driving (MADD), changed California's drunk driving laws, begun a process of legal reforms that would reach all fifty states, caused law enforcement to dramatically increase the number of driving-while-intoxicated (DWI) arrests, and begun the process of greatly reducing the number of DWI deaths each year.

MADD and the DWI reduction provide a wonderful example of how one person can spark a nationwide reform effort. A change in public perception combined with increased law enforcement dramatically improved a major crime problem. The MADD crusade generated an enormous amount of media attention: factual stories, made-for-TV movies, talk-show interviews, and extensive coverage in nearly every national magazine. A more aware public demanded tougher enforcement of tougher laws. More drunk drivers got arrested; those convicted served longer sentences. Slowly, public opinion shifted. Drunk driving was no longer socially acceptable. Millions of social drinkers altered their drinking habits; ultimately, "designated driver" became a common term.

The net effect? A significant decrease in the terrible slaughter on our highways—a trend that shows signs of continued improvement. Even by conservative estimates, at least 140,000 American lives have been saved in the past twenty years by the nationwide change in attitudes about drunk driving.

If we can effect such a reduction in DWI, why not drugs? Drug use rose in the 1970s and remained at high levels during much of the 1980s; in some age groups, more than 50% were using drugs. Popular movies showed drug use as a part of life. In some social circles, it became acceptable and even glamorous.

Then, as dramatically as with DWI, social attitudes changed. In 1987, All-American basketball player Len Bias died from cocaine use. The media noticed. President Reagan and Vice President Bush used the bully pulpit of the White House to lead attacks, creating a cabinet-level drug czar position, filled by William Bennett. Drug arrests rose to more than 1 million per year. Prison sentences, rather than probation, began to more frequently follow convictions. The press became more aggressive in its coverage of drug abuse and the entertainment media stopped glamorizing drugs.

As with DWI, drugs were no longer socially acceptable. The possibility of arrest and conviction increased, and drug usage decreased sharply. In fact, the rate of 37% of young adults using drugs in 1979 declined to 13% in 1992. This decline was caused by an effective combination of prevention and enforcement.

If you are skeptical about such dramatic results, let me propose two other examples. In the 1960s, it became well known that seat belts saved lives and that smoking cost lives. In both cases, massive public education programs coupled with intense media attention changed public opinion. The resulting change in behavior was equally massive.

I, like many other parents, didn't need statistics in order to be aware of these changes. My boys, as preschoolers, were exposed to normal amounts of TV and other media. Like many other parents, if I ever failed to put on my seat belt, I was met with an immediate chorus: "Dad, put on your seat belt!" As for smoking, I once had to intervene as one of my boys, at age 4, launched an explanation of the evils of smoking to some hapless stranger who was lighting up a cigarette in the smoking section of McDonald's.

Seat belts went from being seen as a huge inconvenience to something two thirds of Americans habitually use. Same story with smoking. Between the 1960s and the 1990s, those rates declined from more than 50% of our adult population to barely 25%.

What about some of our other problems? Family violence, the shameful physical and mental abuse which occurs within families, continues to be a social problem of awful proportions. One thing that has changed about this problem, though, is public awareness. And public awareness, as the examples of DWI and drugs have shown, is a powerful catalyst for change.

Indeed, the same cycle that occurred with DWI and drug abuse is now happening with spousal abuse and the other aspects of family violence. Media attention has been high for several years. Entertainment in the form of both Hollywood and TV movies has dramatized its horrors. Talk shows and national magazines continue to devote a lot of airtime and column inches to it. Tougher laws have been passed, and arrests and convictions have both increased.

Family violence may prove to be more difficult to combat than either DWI or drug abuse. Closed doors, increased cohabitation, and a myriad of emotions make monitoring results much more difficult. Yet the efforts to combat such domestic abuse have undoubtedly moderated the problem. In the years to come, we will see whether dramatic changes can be demonstrated.

An offshoot of the trend toward successful combinations of prevention and enforcement is the current emphasis on community policing. The basic concept is sound: by making a uniformed police officer a visible, known person in a community, the community will become stronger, and ultimately crime will be reduced. Although I don't believe, as some do, that community policing is a panacea for all of our social problems, I do believe that the basic idea makes sense; it can cause public attitudes to change. A prevention/enforcement combination succeeds when its targeted criminal conduct is rendered socially unacceptable. In the cases of drug use and DWI, for example, the combined weight of the influences of key leaders, media, and tougher law enforcement practices succeeded in significantly changing public attitudes toward alcohol and drug use. It was no longer cool. Thus, to the degree that community policing results in changed attitudes, it will succeed. The community policing approach may be particularly effective in high-crime neighborhoods, as breaking the law or allowing teenagers to run wild becomes socially unacceptable. At the same time, reporting crimes and becoming involved are likely to become more socially acceptable.

For several more years, the media will assault domestic violence and feature community policing. It is hoped that the earlier successes against DWI and drugs can be repeated in the areas of family violence and neighborhood crime.

VICTIMS' RIGHTS In 1995, I wrote and published *Texas Crime Victims Handbook.* The book could not have been written twenty years earlier because victims simply had no rights.

Karen Kalergis, the former director of the Texas Crime Victim Clearinghouse, summed it up: "Used to be victims of crime had the right to be present at the scene of the crime—and that was that." The late Nell Myers, whose daughter was the victim of a brutal murder, was one of the pioneers in the victims' rights movement in Texas. She can remember when public officials and legislators were not particularly interested in those rights. Nell formed a group called People Against Violent Crime. Nell Myers soon had the attention of all elected officials. Her work led her to, among other places, the Rose Garden of the White House, where she was honored for her work on behalf of victims.

Texas has led the United States in helping victims. Some of our notable achievements include

- the Crime Victim Bill of Rights
- the victim impact statement to give victims a voice in sentencing and parole decisions
- the Crime Victims' Compensation System, which has paid over $500 million in uninsured losses to victims of violent crimes
- legislation requiring criminals to pay back their victims
- a network of victim liaisons in every law enforcement and prosecutor's office
- the Crime Victim Clearinghouse, established to, among other things, provide quality training for crime victim advocates
- a network of rape crisis centers and battered women's shelters

We have a host of other programs and legal rights for victims. The victims' rights movement is thriving in Texas and will continue to influence legislation and command new media attention in the coming years.

These four trends help to place current news stories in perspective. It is only with this perspective that we can understand what we read in our daily newspapers.

While these trends are all positive, there is one dark cloud on the horizon. There is growing pressure, from members of the Texas Legislature and at least one large newspaper, for parole officials to increase parole releases and decrease the number of parole revocations. Also, as the legislature meets in the first half of 2005, there are serious proposals that would allow some lower level offenders to serve shorter prison sentences.

It is impossible to know if this "dark cloud" will develop into a full-blown thunderstorm that will be the next trend in Texas criminal justice. Certainly, if the legislature and state officials either are unwilling to pay the cost for maintaining our current level of incarceration or succumb to the illogical argument that rates of incarceration and crime are not related, then our crime rate will increase. "Increased crime rate" is simply an antiseptic way of saying more Texans will be raped, murdered, robbed, and assaulted and more Texas children will be the victims of abuse.

It is precisely to guard against this possibility that I originally wrote this book in 1997. We all have a stake in an effective criminal justice system. We must understand how broken the system was—and we must resolve not to set a Kenneth McDuff free again.

One way to prevent that horror is to learn about the system and become informed about the issues. This book is my part in that effort. Let's begin our look at the system with its law enforcement officers—people like Jim Boutwell.

C H A P T E R 1

THE SYSTEM: POLICE, PROSECUTORS, JUDGES

Jim Boutwell was a lawman's lawman. During his 44-year career in law enforcement, Jim saw an incredible array of criminals and victims—the best and the worst of human nature. Jim was a Texas Ranger. He piloted an airplane around the University of Texas tower to distract and draw fire from mass murderer Charles Whitman. He talked vicious criminals into giving complete confessions of their crimes. He comforted small children after their mothers were killed.

For the final 15 years of his career, Jim was the sheriff of Williamson County. His tall, thin figure was known throughout the area; it seemed he knew everyone.

Governors and senators confided in Jim; they asked his advice. If citizens walked into Jim's office with a problem, he took the time to listen. He epitomized the old-time Texas sheriff—tough, soft-spoken, part public figure, part psychologist, part social worker—a lawman from the tip of his Stetson to the soles of his cowboy boots.

Perhaps no sheriff and district attorney had a closer working relationship than Jim and I had. We talked on the phone daily and, more often than not, drank a cup of coffee together. We had a common purpose. We believed we really could make Williamson County a safer, better place for our neighbors to live in.

At the L&M Cafe on Austin Avenue in downtown Georgetown, Jim and I did some of our best work. We painstakingly pieced together circumstantial murder cases. We debated the next step of an investigation. We planned undercover operations against burglars and drug dealers. Early in the movement for victims' rights, we put together a unit to help victims of crime and to serve as a model for other counties. The downfall of more than one criminal doing life in the state prison system began with an investigation put together on a coffee-stained napkin at the L&M Cafe.

The Crestview Baptist Church was packed on the day of Jim's funeral in November 1993. At 66, Jim had lost his battle with cancer. From my front row seat with the other pallbearers, I stared at the casket and, on the table next to it, four items: Jim's Smith and Wesson, his leather holster, his Stetson, and his badge. I had lost a good friend. Texas had lost a good law officer.

As a district attorney, I had the pleasure of working with many first-rate police officers, some truly dedicated prosecutors, and some great judges. Indeed, my views of all such officials are strongly influenced by the memory of Jim Boutwell. I admire and respect all the Jim Boutwells of this world.

But I am also aware of the other kind. The headlines have told their stories—the West Texas sheriff sent to prison for drug dealing; the Fort Bend County district attorney removed from office for revealing confidential grand jury testimony about a political enemy; the Galveston County judge caught on camera sleeping during a trial. When I think about Jim Boutwell and the many other fine law enforcement officers I've known and worked with, cases like these are hard to understand. But my own case files show the convictions and prison sentences for a half-dozen or so officers gone bad—for bribery, drugs, child molesting.

As you read this chapter, the grim statistics about police officer fatalities may sadden you. It may outrage you to read about the technical grounds on which some criminals get new trials. But amid the statistics and the emotions, we need to understand something. We all have a stake in having the right people in these jobs. We need more Jim Boutwells and fewer who are willing to violate the public trust.

I'll leave the platitudes to the civics teachers, but to get the right people into these jobs, we need to educate ourselves by asking, "What do these jobs require of those who do them?"

LAW ENFORCEMENT OFFICERS For citizens, the most visible people in the system are law enforcement officers. Texas has roughly 80,000 of them. Some are local officers who get their paychecks from the city or county. Others get their paychecks from the state. They enforce laws and investigate crimes.

DANGEROUS WORK

The names of 1,112 law officers who gave their lives protecting us are carved in the black granite memorial on the grounds of the State Capitol in Austin. The semicircular granite wall is part of the Texas Peace Officers Memorial—authorized by the Texas Legislature and paid for with private donations. The first officer to die was Bexar County sheriff J. L. Hood, who was killed by Indians on March 19, 1840.

Law enforcement work has always been physically tough and emotionally draining. It remains dangerous today. Roughly 5,000 officers are assaulted in the line of duty each year.

Texas has frequently led the nation in officer fatalities. During the past 10 years, 105 officers were killed. Fifty-three of them died by criminal acts. The others were killed by accidental means—usually while driving or directing traffic.

QUALIFICATIONS Law enforcement officers have many different titles, but they must be peace officers; that is, they must be licensed by the state. Their licensing agency, the Texas Commission on Law Enforcement Officer Standards and Education, requires

- U.S. citizenship
- 21 years of age (with some exceptions)
- good moral character
- no felony convictions
- physical and mental fitness

Men and women who qualify must complete a 560-hour training course and pass a written examination.

LOCAL OFFICERS Incorporated cities have police departments. Their police officers answer calls and investigate crimes within the geographical limits of their city.

In unincorporated portions of Texas counties and in the very small towns, sheriffs and their deputies answer calls and investigate crimes. Each of the 254 Texas counties has a sheriff.

A number of other local law officers—airport police, school district police, park police, and constables—may provide limited law enforcement services in their areas.

STATE OFFICERS Some agencies operate statewide. Their officers either actively look for criminal activity or help local officers.

The largest group of state officers works for the Department of Public Safety. Its Highway Patrol Division enforces traffic laws and investigates traffic accidents. The best-known statewide group, the Texas Rangers, helps local agencies with complex investigations such as homicides and political corruption. Other large statewide agencies with law enforcement officers are the Parks and Wildlife Department and the Alcoholic Beverage Commission.

TEXAS RANGERS

The Texas Rangers are like a very few other well-known agencies: Scotland Yard, the Royal Canadian Mounted Police, the FBI. For these law enforcement agencies, legends are natural. Because of their Wild West tradition, the Rangers have been the subject of numerous books, movies, and TV shows. They enjoy a worldwide reputation.

The Rangers were first organized in 1823 when Stephen F. Austin felt that his fledgling colony of settlers needed additional protection against the native population. Austin hired 10 men to "act as rangers for the common defense." They were paid $15 a month (in land) and had to supply their own horses and guns.

For the past 181 years, the Rangers have existed in some form as a protective force. Although their history has included some dark moments, their overall record is one of courage and strength. They fought American Indians, chased outlaws out of South Texas, and captured bank robbers like John Wesley Hardin and killers like Bonnie and Clyde.

Today, the Texas Rangers are 118 investigators who operate statewide. Primarily, they help local police and sheriffs solve major crimes—particularly homicides and political corruption. Yes, today's Rangers are much more likely to jump on a helicopter than a horse and to log on to a computer than to strap on a six-shooter. But the Rangers are still pretty much what Stephen F. Austin envisioned—an efficient, courageous group of law officers who provide extra protection for Texas citizens.

PROSECUTORS Prosecutors represent the State of Texas in criminal cases. Most people know what prosecutors do in a courtroom.

They question witnesses and argue in front of juries. But prosecutors do a lot of work outside the courtroom. They

- review police reports
- review scientific reports
- review the defendant's criminal history
- present the case to a grand jury
- prepare an indictment
- discuss the case with the defense attorney
- discuss the case with the investigator
- discuss the case with the victim
- interview witnesses
- visit the crime scene
- research legal issues likely to be raised by the defense

Only after this preparation can prosecutors fully understand the crime and the criminal and represent the state's interests in court. Prosecution offices in Texas include

- district attorneys
- county attorneys
- criminal district attorneys
- city attorneys

They prosecute cases in the district, county, municipal, and justice of the peace courts.

DISTRICT ATTORNEYS District attorneys

- prosecute criminal cases in district court
- represent the state when someone appeals a conviction
- advise law enforcement agencies
- present cases to the grand jury
- conduct certain specialized criminal investigations
- represent the state in asset forfeitures, such as taking profits away from a drug dealer
- represent the state in felony bond forfeitures
- provide victim services

District attorneys' offices, created by the legislature, each serve one or more counties and are funded primarily by them. District attorneys are elected for 4 years by the voters of the area they serve. District attorneys hire all assistant district attorneys and the rest of their staffs.

MR. DISTRICT ATTORNEY

For many Texans over 40, it is difficult to hear the word "district attorney" without the name Henry Wade coming to mind.

Wade served as the tough, no-nonsense district attorney of Dallas County for thirty-six years, from 1950 to 1986. A former FBI agent and combat veteran, he had a career that included more than two dozen capital murder convictions and the lead role in the 1964 prosecution of Jack Ruby for the murder of presidential assassin Lee Harvey Oswald.

Wade ran a tight ship; his prosecutors were known for their white shirts, dark blue suits, short haircuts, and high conviction rates. He was also an innovator. The prosecutor training he offered in his office was open to prosecutors throughout Texas and his Career Criminal and Victim/Witness divisions were studied and copied by district attorneys throughout the nation.

Of course, other district attorneys, through leadership, innovation, and longevity, also deserve the title "Mr. District Attorney." Two first-rate prosecutors, Carol Vance (Harris County, 1966–1979) and Arthur "Cappy" Eads (Bell County, 1977–2000), served as presidents of the National District Attorneys Association. Johnny Holmes (Harris County, 1980–2000) was colorful, outspoken, and effective; his office obtained more death penalty sentences than any other in the country. The current record for longevity belongs to Tim Curry, who for over thirty years has been district attorney of Tarrant County.

COUNTY ATTORNEYS County attorneys

- prosecute misdemeanor criminal cases
- represent the state in appeals of these convictions
- advise law enforcement agencies
- represent the state in misdemeanor bond-forfeiture cases
- provide victim services
- provide legal services to county government

Most county attorneys have active programs for collecting hot checks. Each year, these programs return tens of millions of dollars to victims. County attorneys, elected every 4 years, serve only a single county. In rural areas, their position may only be part-time. The office is funded by the local county government.

CRIMINAL DISTRICT ATTORNEYS Criminal district attorneys prosecute both felonies and misdemeanors, thus combining the criminal prosecution functions of both the county and district attorney in one office. A county's voters elect criminal district attorneys to 4-year terms. Their offices, created by the legislature, are funded primarily by the county they serve.

CITY ATTORNEYS City attorneys, who are hired by city governments, prosecute criminal cases in municipal court. In larger cities, the city attorney hires assistants. In smaller cities and towns, the city attorney is a local lawyer who prosecutes cases part-time.

COURTS The legislature has created two types of courts: trial and appeal. It also has determined the number and locations of each type. Each has a set jurisdiction, that is, a list of the types of cases it may hear. Texas has five levels of trial courts and two levels of appeals courts.

Criminal Trial Courts

- justice of the peace courts
- municipal courts
- county courts
- county courts at law
- district courts

Criminal Appeals Courts

- courts of appeals
- court of criminal appeals

CRIMINAL TRIAL COURTS

Justice of the Peace Courts Every county in Texas has a justice of the peace court to hear civil and criminal cases where the maximum punishment is a fine that does not exceed $500. These crimes, Class C misdemeanors, include theft under $50, gambling, writing a hot check, and disorderly conduct.

Justices of the peace do not have to be lawyers. Only in Texas' half-dozen largest counties are all JPs lawyers. In the rest of the state, only about 20% of JPs are lawyers. In addition to hearing Class C misdemeanors, JPs also

- set bonds
- arraign defendants
- issue most search warrants
- issue arrest warrants
- hear bond forfeitures in their criminal cases
- determine cause of death in those Texas counties that don't have a medical examiner

The first four duties (bonds, arraignments, search warrants, arrest warrants) can be performed by any "magistrate." A magistrate can be any judge in Texas. As a practical matter, these duties are almost always performed by the justices of the peace, by municipal judges or, in a few larger counties, by specially appointed magistrates or court masters.

Municipal Courts Any incorporated city, town, or village may create a municipal court. Such a court has no civil jurisdiction but has criminal jurisdiction similar to that of a justice of the peace court.

Municipal courts may hear criminal cases that occur within the legal limits of their city or town. Their jurisdiction involves crimes that carry a fine only where the fine does not exceed $500 (Class C misdemeanors). Municipal courts may also hear criminal cases under a city ordinance (such as a fire-code or health-code violation) where the fine does not exceed $2,000. Municipal judges are also magistrates. That means they can arraign defendants, set bonds, and issue search and arrest warrants.

Appeals from municipal court are to the county-level court. A complete new trial, called a *trial de novo,* is held there. A few municipal courts are designated as courts of record. In these courts, a complete written record must be made of everything that happens at the trial. Instead of a trial de novo, an appeal based on this written record goes to a special appellate court or a county-level court. A further appeal can be made directly to the Court of Appeals.

Municipal judges are either elected or appointed as established by the legislature and the local city government. The city's governing body sets the qualifications for their judges.

County Courts Each of the 254 counties in Texas has a county judge. In addition to traditional judges' duties, the county judges run their counties. That is, they serve more or less as the mayor and chief administrator.

The county judge hears misdemeanors where jail time is a possible punishment. These Class A and B misdemeanors include driving while intoxicated (first and second offense), theft between $50 and $1,500, unlawful carrying of a weapon, possession and delivery of small amounts of marijuana, and some lesser types of assault.

In addition, county judges hear appeals from justice of the peace courts and municipal courts. County judges are also magistrates, and they have the same jursidiction as the justices of the peace to set bonds, arraign defendants, and issue search and arrest warrants, although normally they do not perform these duties. County judges do not have to be lawyers. The vast majority of them, even in urban areas, are not.

County Courts at Law Most Texans live in counties where the county judge performs very few, if any, judicial duties. In these counties, the county judge will preside at meetings of the commissioners' court and manage the county. The judicial duties will be performed by a county court at law judge.

Texas has 212 county courts at law, created by the legislature. The law that creates them sets out their individual duties. These duties vary from court to court, but they have some or all of the county court's duties.

County court at law judges must be lawyers. They also may have additional qualifications set by the legislature.

District Courts Texas has 425 district courts to hear felony criminal cases. Felonies, the most serious types of crimes, include murder, robbery, sexual assault, and most drug offenses. District courts also hear misdemeanor cases that involve official misconduct.

District courts are organized by counties or groups of counties. The legislature determines the number of district courts in each county or, in rural areas, the number of counties served by a single district court. Most district courts hear both civil and criminal cases. In metropolitan areas, some district courts specialize and hear exclusively criminal cases or exclusively one or more types of civil cases.

As do other courts, district courts have duties relating to their criminal cases. The judges can hear bond forfeitures from cases in their courts. They also are magistrates with the power to conduct arraignments, set bonds, and issue search and arrest warrants. District judges can issue search warrants for law enforcement officers to obtain evidence. District judges also have jurisdiction over asset forfeiture cases. These cases take from the criminal the items used to commit a crime or the profits from a crime.

District judges must be lawyers. They must have practiced law for 2 years, but they have no age requirement. The voters of the county or counties they serve elect them for a 4-year term.

District Court Magistrates Five large counties—Bexar, Dallas, Lubbock, Tarrant, and Travis—have district court magistrates. These magistrates, appointed by the district judges, perform many of the same duties as district judges except they do not conduct actual trials.

CRIMINAL APPEALS COURTS An appeals court reviews the trial record, the written recording of what was said and done in court. This review will determine whether the trial judge, prosecutor, or jury did anything improper that in some way denied the defendant a fair trial.

Texas has two types of criminal appeals courts—the Court of Appeals and the Court of Criminal Appeals. The Court of Criminal Appeals is the highest criminal court in Texas. The Texas Supreme Court does not hear criminal cases.

Courts of Appeals Each of these 14 courts has a minimum of 3 judges. They must be at least 35 years old and have practiced law for 10 years. The voters in the region of the state they serve elect them to 6-year terms. These courts, each serving many counties, are in Houston (two courts), Fort Worth, Austin, San Antonio, Dallas, Texarkana, Amarillo, El Paso, Beaumont, Waco, Eastland, Tyler, and Corpus Christi.

Courts of appeals hear all appeals from county and district courts, except for death penalty cases. In reviewing the trial, the judges on the court will review the record and the written or oral arguments from attorneys. They do not hear witnesses.

In deciding criminal appeals, a court of appeals has three choices. Most convictions, it upholds. Occasionally, it reverses the conviction and orders a new trial. For a very few, it decides that the evidence against the defendant was so weak that it orders him or her found "not guilty." No retrial is allowed.

Court of Criminal Appeals This court has 9 judges elected on a statewide basis for 6-year terms. They must be at least 35 years old and have practiced law for 10 years.

This court hears all death penalty appeals. It also may—but doesn't have to—review cases which have been decided by the courts of appeals to clear up confusion in the law or when it feels the case will affect a number of other cases. If it decides the court of appeals was wrong, it can change that decision.

The only appeal from a Court of Criminal Appeals decision is to the United States Supreme Court. The Supreme Court hears only a very few criminal cases each year. Because Texas has so many death penalty cases, it is not unusual for a Texas case to be heard by the Supreme Court each year. However, in a whole decade, the Supreme Court may hear only one or two non–death penalty cases from Texas.

TECHNICAL REVERSALS

Appeals courts have the difficult job of reviewing records from trials to determine whether the trial judge or prosecutor made any mistakes that caused the trial not to be fair. As a trial judge and former prosecutor, I understand and accept the need to have such a review. However, sometimes appeals courts order new trials because of technical mistakes—mistakes that have nothing to do with the fairness of the trial or whether the defendant was innocent. Consider Tracy Gee.

Tracy was bright, honest, family oriented. She loved kids and was always ready to help others. The 22-year-old Houstonian, the youngest of eight sisters, had career aspirations to be an architect or interior designer.

In September 1990, Tracy was working as an assistant pro shop manager at The City Club. She worked a double shift, filling in for her sister who was on maternity leave, and left work shortly after midnight on September 5.

Meanwhile, Lionell Rodriguez and his cousin James were cruising the streets of Houston armed with both a shotgun and an automatic rifle. They decided to rob an Exxon station but gave up because there were too many customers. They then drove around talking about robberies.

Sometime later they stopped at a stoplight next to Tracy Gee's Honda. Lionell Rodriguez saw Tracy. He took his rifle, aimed it at her head, and fired a fatal shot. He then ran to the driver's side of the Honda, broke out the glass, unlocked the car, pulled Tracy's body into the street, and took her car.

Lionell Rodriguez was arrested a few hours later, still driving Tracy's Honda. He confessed. A Harris County jury convicted him and sentenced him to death.

On appeal, Rodriguez claimed that he deserved a new trial because, when the original jury was being picked, the trial judge twice allowed a small portion of it to be shuffled (the names put into a hat and randomly drawn in the order they would be considered). Incredibly, five of the nine judges on the Court of Criminal Appeals agreed that this "error" required an automatic retrial of the entire case.

It was a shocking miscarriage of justice. Rodriguez was given a new trial—not because he might be innocent, not because his trial wasn't fair, but because of a very insignificant technical error. Of course, Tracy's family and loved ones had to endure a second trial. At the second trial, Rodriguez was again convicted and sentenced to death.

Unfortunately, this injustice is not limited to just one case. Here are some other recent examples.

Aaron Stine had his 20-year prison sentence for aggravated assault overturned and a new trial was ordered. Why? Well, Stine had been tried in Meridian, the county seat of Bosque County. He'd wanted a speedy trial because he was afraid the victim might die and the charges might be upgraded to murder. So with Stine's consent, the trial had been partially held in the victim's hospital room ten miles away in the town of Clifton. The new trial was ordered because a majority of the Court of Criminal Appeals held that it was automatically improper to try a case outside of the county seat.

Eva Morales had her drug conviction and prison sentence overturned and a new trial ordered even though she pled guilty. Why? Well, during the often-hectic days in court, the trial judge had forgotten to tell Eva, as the law requires, that if she were not a United States citizen a conviction might affect her immigration status. The majority of the Court of Criminal Appeals held that Morales was entitled to an automatic new trial even though no evidence showed that she was not a United States citizen.

Presiding Judge Mike McCormick, who voted to uphold the convictions of each of the above defendants, was outraged by the decisions of his colleagues on the Court of Criminal Appeals. He termed one of the rulings "another triumph of narrow technicalities over practical common sense."

Fortunately, Texas voters were sufficiently outraged by these decisions that they put an end to them by electing judges who agreed with Judge McCormick that "common sense" was more important than "narrow technicalities." For the past eight years, the "technical reversals" have stopped and cases are only being reversed where the court finds a significant error that affected the fairness of the trial.

FEDERAL SYSTEM This book tells you about the Texas criminal justice system. Most crime is investigated by local agencies and prosecuted by state prosecutors in local county courthouses. It is this system that a citizen needs to understand.

However, a brief description of the federal system will help you better understand the Texas system. It also will help to avoid confusion since the news media often fail to make clear which system a particular case arose in.

The federal government maintains a criminal justice system completely distinct from a state's. The federal system has its own investigators, prosecutors, judges, and courthouses. Federal prisons hold about one-tenth the number of prisoners of all the states' prisons combined.

The federal system divides Texas into 4 districts. Prosecution in each district is led by the United States attorney for that district. This attorney is appointed by the President and confirmed by the United States Senate. A U.S. attorney serves at the pleasure of the President and is usually replaced when a new president takes office.

Federal judges are appointed for life by the President and also confirmed by the Senate.

In Texas, you'll find federal courthouses and United States attorneys' offices in most of the larger cities:

- Northern District: Amarillo, Dallas, Fort Worth, and Lubbock
- Eastern District: Beaumont, Sherman, and Tyler
- Western District: Austin, Del Rio, El Paso, Midland, Pecos, San Antonio, and Waco
- Southern District: Brownsville, Corpus Christi, Houston, and Laredo

Crimes prosecuted in federal court are usually the result of a federal investigation by one of the following agencies:

- Federal Bureau of Investigation
- Secret Service
- United States Customs
- Alcohol, Tobacco and Firearms
- Drug Enforcement Administration
- Postal Inspectors
- Internal Revenue Service

Most cases prosecuted in the federal system are white-collar crimes, large drug cases, or firearms violations. Occasionally, a bank robbery or a case involving an armed career criminal may be prosecuted in federal court.

There are no clear rules for which system prosecutes which crime. Crimes investigated by federal agencies are sometimes prosecuted in state court. Crimes investigated by state agencies are sometimes prosecuted in federal court. It depends on local cooperation and practices between the United States attorney, the local district attorney, and the agency investigating the crime.

Other than these structural and name differences, the federal and state systems operate in a similar manner. The major operating difference is in sentencing.

Federal judges always do the sentencing, never a jury, and they must sentence according to very narrow guidelines established by Congress. Several years ago, Congress did away with parole for federal sentences. Except for a small deduction for good behavior, prisoners must serve their entire sentences.

This chapter has laid the foundation for understanding the Texas criminal justice system. It has provided a sense of the duties of law enforcement officers, prosecutors, and judges, along with an outline of both the state and federal court system. With this foundation, we can now move to the actual operation of the system—the rules which govern investigations, arrests, trials, and appeals. We will begin our story at a downtown Austin restaurant.

CHAPTER 2

CRIMINAL PROCEDURE

One of downtown Austin's trendy restaurants is the City Grill on Sabine Street. The morning I visited, it wasn't yet open for lunch. Rather than sitting in the dining room, I stood over a stack of produce crates. I wasn't there to eat. I was looking through invoices to answer a question. What vegetables had been on the menu the night of August 12? Had those vegetables then turned up in a murder victim's stomach?

So much for the glamour of being a trial lawyer.

As a kid growing up, I got my ideas about trials and lawyers from movies, TV, and books. Gregory Peck in *To Kill a Mockingbird.* Spencer Tracy in *Inherit the Wind.* In the popular media, the "good-guy" lawyer is always handsome or beautiful, always a star in the courtroom, always able to break down any lying witness with a brilliant cross-examination. And always able to expose the truth.

In reality, I don't see much brilliance in the courtroom. Trials are won and the truth is exposed because of detailed, painstaking preparation done before the first witness is sworn in. Someone has to visit the crime scene, interview the witnesses, retrace the steps of the victim or defendant, and examine the physical evidence. Someone has to master the hundreds of details.

Such preparation led me to the produce crates at the City Grill. A neighbor discovered a young mother murdered in her bed. Her husband was off at work. His story, that she was alive when he left for work at 5:30 A.M., didn't fit with the evidence. Ultimately, he was indicted for her murder.

The defendant and his wife had celebrated his birthday the night before at the City Grill. My theory of the crime was that after returning home, he wanted to have sex. When she said no, he savagely beat her to death. A critical part of the proof was the results of the autopsy; the medical examiner fixed her time of death at around midnight but no later than 4 A.M. This time of death was fixed in part by the wife's stomach contents. The food there was only partially digested. I could see and easily identify pieces of mushrooms, squash, olives, and tomatoes.

Two weeks before trial, I visited the City Grill. The waitress who had served the couple found their dinner ticket. The wife's order matched her stomach contents, except for the vegetable side dish. It changed nightly depending on the produce available and delivered to the kitchen. So there I was, going through produce invoices with the manager. We found the correct date and, sure enough, the vegetable side dish that night had included mushrooms, squash, olives, and tomatoes.

We also knew that the defense team—three very capable lawyers—would call their own expert witness to cast doubt on the medical examiner's conclusion. I didn't want the jury to lose the significance of this evidence because of a clash between experts and a bunch of medical jargon. So I asked the City Grill manager to re-create the victim's last meal and bring it to court.

On the issue of time of death, the defense lawyers did their job. Two experts testified, throwing around—as expected—a lot of confusing, highly technical jargon about medical studies.

On rebuttal, I called the City Grill manager and produced a still-warm plate duplicating the exact meal the victim had eaten. The impact on the jury was clear; the meal looked much like the stomach contents the medical examiner had described. It was a very effective demonstration. It wasn't brilliance; it was simple preparation and attention to detail. The defendant was convicted and is currently serving a life sentence for killing his wife.

This chapter tells you about criminal procedure, the rules for investigations and trials. At times, these rules may seem overly technical or dull—certainly not the stuff of the courtroom drama we can't get enough of on TV.

But the rules provide truthful and accurate information in court. They protect basic liberties at the core of American government. Law enforcement officials and prosecutors must master these rules in order to make our homes and neighborhoods safer.

Moreover, every Texas citizen can use an understanding of these rules to make sense of the headlines and understand what happens in criminal cases.

INVESTIGATION A criminal case begins when a crime becomes known to a law enforcement agency. A citizen can report a crime or a law enforcement officer can observe a crime. Whenever a law enforcement agency becomes aware of a crime, some form of investigation takes place. The agency may simply record a citizen's complaint. Or it may do a full-scale investigation that takes lots of time and dozens of officers using sophisticated techniques.

As a general rule, the greater the seriousness of the crime and the greater the probability of its being solved, the greater the intensity of the investigation. For example, what about a hot check with no leads on locating the person who wrote the check? This type of crime is not likely to be investigated beyond filing a report. But homicides are vigorously investigated—at least while there are leads worth pursuing.

Law enforcement officers investigate on three levels at the same time.

1. They must follow proper *legal procedures* while they gather evidence so that the courts can accept it.
2. They must follow proper *scientific procedures* while they gather evidence so that the crime lab can properly analyze it.
3. They must follow *deductive procedures* while they analyze evidence so that they can determine who committed the crime.

LEGAL PROCEDURES The U.S. Constitution's Bill of Rights, the Texas Constitution, and laws passed by the Texas Legislature restrict investigations. These restrictions limit the power of government and protect an individual person's rights.

THE BILL OF RIGHTS

When the United States Constitution was proposed and being debated, its critics had strong points. One was its failure to enumerate the rights of citizens. Although it was ratified by the required 9 of 13 states by mid-1788, one of Congress's first actions was to propose 10 amendments which constitute the Bill of Rights. These amendments were ratified by 11 of the 14 states and became part of the Constitution in 1791.

These amendments, particularly the Fourth, Fifth, Sixth, and Eighth and sometimes the First, are frequently used in criminal cases to protect the rights of an accused citizen. They are, of course, the basic document that protects the freedoms of law-abiding citizens, also.

First Amendment: **Protects freedom of religion, speech, and press.**

Second Amendment: **Protects the right to bear arms.**

Third Amendment: **Prohibits the U.S. government from forcibly quartering troops in a private home.**

Fourth Amendment: **Prohibits unreasonable searches and seizures.**

Fifth Amendment: **Requires grand jury indictment, prohibits double-jeopardy and self-incrimination, and requires due process of law.**

Sixth Amendment: **Guarantees an accused citizen the right to a speedy public trial, an impartial jury, and advance knowledge of the charges. It also guarantees the right of the accused to confront opposing witnesses, to obtain favorable witnesses' presence at trial, and to have a lawyer.**

Seventh Amendment: **Guarantees right to a jury trial for civil suits involving more than $20.**

Eighth Amendment: **Prohibits excessive bail and cruel and unusual punishments.**

Ninth Amendment: **Recognizes that other rights not specifically set out are retained by the people.**

Tenth Amendment: **Reserves rights, not specifically given to the federal government, for the states or people.**

We often refer to these restrictions by the name of the amendment which mentions them. Fourth Amendment restrictions on searches have the biggest impact on police investigations. While investigating a crime, law officers cannot unreasonably search you, your home, or your car. They cannot unreasonably take your property away from you. But what does unreasonable mean?

As a very general rule, the officers must obtain a search warrant before searching private property. However, many exceptions let the officers search without warrants when it would not be practical to get one.

A search warrant is a piece of paper, signed by a judge, that lets law officers search a specific place for specific items. The officers must, in a sworn statement, explain to the judge why they want to search that place. These reasons must convince the judge of probable cause. That is, for a search to be reasonable, the judge must believe that, on the basis of all the evidence, it is likely that a piece of evidence is at a certain place.

Search warrants, especially the sworn statement to the judge, must meet many legal requirements. It usually takes an hour or more to prepare such a statement. Law enforcement officers frequently ask prosecutors for help, which takes additional time. The time delays involved in preparing search warrants are not practical for many situations. For example, the criminal suspect could simply destroy the evidence while the police were off obtaining the warrant. So in many cases, the officers are not required to obtain a search warrant to immediately search and then to seize evidence that they find. But they must still have probable cause because a judge will later evaluate the grounds for the search.

Here's the most frequent exception to the search warrant requirement. When officers make a lawful arrest, they usually search the person arrested and any area the person could immediately reach. This search reasonably protects the officers from guns or other weapons and keeps the person arrested from destroying evidence. Another frequent exception is the motor vehicle search. Because of the mobility of motor vehicles, courts allow officers without warrants to search whenever they arrest a driver or passenger or have probable cause to believe evidence is in the vehicle. Of course, officers don't need a warrant when a person with control of the property consents to the search. Such consent may be oral or written.

In many other situations, the officers do not need search warrants. For example, officers may search in schools or workplaces, and they may "search" for items in plain view. Inventory searches, emergency searches, and investigative stop-and-frisks are other examples where the officers do not need search warrants. Despite these many exceptions, a great many search warrants are obtained. Searches of private residences are nearly always conducted under the authority of a search warrant.

Law enforcement officers must also follow certain procedures so that they don't violate a suspect's right to protection against self-incrimination. The officers are free to talk with anyone they think may have information about a case. Or they may have a co-defendant or informer contact a suspect about a crime.

Law officers must give Miranda warnings to anyone they arrest or, during questioning, to anyone they suspect of a crime. After that warning, any voluntary statement the suspects make can be used against them in court. Miranda warnings also tell the suspects about important rights:

- the right to remain silent
- the right for a lawyer to be present during any questioning
- the right to an appointed lawyer

Officers do not have to use a prescribed set of words. As a practical matter, most officers carry a card with the Miranda warnings printed on it. To ensure that there is later no question about the suspects having been warned, officers frequently have them initial the card or each of the specific rights separately.

After these warnings are given and the suspects waive their rights, it is perfectly proper procedure for an officer to question them at length. The officer can show the suspects inconsistencies in their stories or confront them with evidence linking them to the crime.

If the suspects wish to confess, they must either write out their confession or record it on an audio or video recorder. Each type of situation has particular technical requirements; in the case of a confession, for example, the Miranda warnings must appear either in the written statement or on the tape. If an officer fails to follow these legal procedures, the evidence gathered may be excluded from the trial. It is, therefore, essential that an officer know and follow correct legal procedures.

WHAT EXACTLY IS A MIRANDA?

Every American child who has ever turned on a TV set knows the "Miranda" warning. "You have the right to remain silent . . ." But where did the name "Miranda" come from?

In astronomy, stars, comets, and such are named after the scientists who discovered them. In criminal law, it would make sense to name things after legal scholars or distinguished judges. However, in a bizarre twist of logic, we frequently name them after criminals.

The name Miranda comes from Ernesto Miranda, a grade-school dropout who was a small-time thug in Phoenix, Arizona. In 1963, Miranda kidnapped and raped a retarded teenage girl. After he was arrested, he was questioned by police for two hours before he gave a written statement. The police never warned him of his right to remain silent or to have a lawyer.

Miranda was tried, convicted, and sentenced to 20 years in prison. The case was appealed all the way to the United States Supreme Court, which, in 1966, issued its landmark ruling requiring the now-famous warning and setting aside Miranda's conviction.

The local prosecutors back in Phoenix weren't amused. They retried Miranda without using his confession and again obtained a conviction and prison sentence. Miranda was paroled in 1972, continued his life of crime, and spent most of the next four years locked up. In 1976, he met his demise when he was stabbed to death in a bar.

Ernesto Miranda was no hero. He was simply a two-bit thug and rapist who died at age 34 in a barroom fight.

SCIENTIFIC PROCEDURES Crime labs can produce spectacular results when they apply the latest scientific technology to evidence gathered in criminal cases. Some of this technology was not available even five or ten years ago. For example, you see a clean surface at a crime scene. The officers can treat that surface with chemicals, develop a previously unseen bloody fingerprint, and within days have the name of the person who left it. Similarly, with DNA technology, officers can identify a suspect who leaves any biological material at a crime scene, even a single hair or small amounts of blood.

AN "UNSOLVED" CASE: DNA AT WORK

It is every parent's worst nightmare. Three-year-old Cristy Ryno was sleeping on the couch of her apartment with her twin sister. Sometime before her mother woke up on the morning of April 17, 1999, she disappeared. Police were called. A massive search ensued. Tracking dogs lost Cristy's scent just outside her apartment. There simply were no clues.

Cristy's nude body was discovered four days later along the Elm Fork of the Trinity River. She had been sexually assaulted. There was some DNA recovered from her body which likely came from her killer. That DNA was checked against all the adults living in Cristy's apartment. No match. Irving police interviewed every possible adult connected to either Cristy or the apartment complex—three hundred people in all. Still no suspects.

The investigation dragged on for years. Finally, Irving police decided to reinterview the three hundred people connected to the case and request voluntary samples of their DNA.

It was hard, painstaking police work to conduct the reinterviews and gather as many voluntary samples as possible. But it paid off. Over three years later, there was a DNA match. Brett Bednarek, a 26-year-old maintenance man, was arrested for Cristy's murder on July 11, 2002. A year later he was sitting in prison with convictions for both murder and aggravated sexual assault. His sentences were life and 99 years. He must serve 30 calendar years before he is first eligible for parole.

However, none of this technology helps unless the officers follow strict rules when gathering the evidence and submitting it to the lab. The officers must properly document the evidence they seize. Their written reports must note where, when, and under what circumstances they seized it. Often, they will photograph an item such as a bullet casing before they touch it.

The officers must then mark the evidence so that they can identify it at a later time. Usually, they scratch their initials or badge number into the item. Or they put the item in a sealed container and mark the outside of the container. The officers must then ensure that no one tampers with the evidence until it gets to the crime lab. Usually, they put it in a secure evidence room at the police station.

In many cases, they must collect evidence in a special manner. For example, after a sexual assault, the victim must go to a hospital for an examination and for samples of hair, blood, semen, and so on.

In a firearm assault case, the officers often conduct gunshot residue tests on the hands of a possible suspect. After pouring a chemical solution on five hand swabs, they use one swab each to get a sample from the palm and back of both the right and left hands. They don't do anything with the fifth swab, which serves as a control sample. All of these samples must be properly taken, documented, and submitted to the crime lab. For certain types of evidence, such as bite marks, officers must place a ruler or other reference next to them for the photograph.

In short, many cases require special knowledge by the law enforcement officers who gather the evidence. Failure to follow these procedures can eliminate or greatly reduce the value of important evidence.

DEDUCTIVE PROCEDURES Keeping these legal and scientific procedures in mind, the law enforcement officers must analyze the evidence and solve the crime. From all the evidence, they make a logical deduction about who committed the crime.

Despite the incredible scientific breakthroughs in the crime lab, many crimes are still solved by tips. Tips may come from more or less regular police sources or from anonymous sources such as a Crime Stoppers program. Crime Stoppers and other reward programs work well.

CRIME STOPPERS: A PROGRAM THAT WORKS

Crime Stoppers is one of the most successful anticrime programs in the nation. It began as a local program in Albuquerque, New Mexico, in 1976. Its success there led to its adoption throughout the United States.

Crime Stoppers programs center around a hotline phone number for people to anonymously call in information on unsolved crimes. If the information leads to an arrest or indictment, the anonymous informant can collect a reward of up to $1,000.

Crime Stoppers is the only anticrime program that relies on private citizens to run it, raise money for it, and pay the rewards. Reward money comes from private donations.

In Texas, Crime Stoppers programs began in the early 1980s. A statewide coordinating agency certifies and coordinates many of the local programs. We now have 110 certified local programs and approximately 30 uncertified programs.

Since its inception, Texas Crime Stoppers programs were directly responsible for the arrest of more than 80,000 suspects, recovery of $149 million in stolen property, and seizure of hundreds of millions of dollars worth of illegal narcotics. An astonishing 96% of the suspects arrested through Crime Stoppers have been convicted.

Each local program has its own hotline number. However, information can also be reported to the 24-hour statewide hotline at 1–800–252–TIPS.

Law enforcement agencies also help each other. Many crimes are solved when one agency makes an arrest and shares information with another agency. For example, one agency arrests a burglar coming out of a house. A follow-up investigation may reveal stolen goods in the burglar's home which can help another agency solve a related burglary.

Computer technology helps, too. In 1992, Texas started using a $22-million computerized fingerprint system. The Automated Fingerprint Identification System (AFIS) checks fingerprints against the Department of Public Safety's master fingerprint file. AFIS works even with only part of a single fingerprint. Each year AFIS solves over 2,000 serious crimes that might have gone unsolved using traditional methods. This computerized fingerprint technology will become even more effective in coming years as a national AFIS system (named IAFIS, the "I" standing for "integrated") comes online.

AFIS IN ACTION

Someone burglarized a church in downtown San Angelo. Police department investigators searched the crime scene and found numerous latent fingerprints, including some at the

point of entry. The following day, the investigators entered the prints into AFIS and received a match. The suspect was otherwise unknown to them. His prints came from his 1990 arrest for driving without a license. While the investigators were processing these prints, a second church burglary was reported. The crime scene gave investigators many more fingerprints. A quick check confirmed that it was the same burglar. The next afternoon, they arrested the burglar and recovered the property from both burglaries.

The AFIS success is being replicated with other computer database matching systems. The Combined DNA Index System (CODIS) allows the known DNA of convicted offenders to be matched with offenders' DNA from unsolved sexual assaults, murders, and other violent crimes, especially cases with little likelihood of being solved. The system will become more effective as more known DNA profiles are added to the database. Currently 10 to 20 cases per month are being solved by CODIS. These "cold hits" are resulting in the arrest and conviction of killers and rapists. As with AFIS, a National DNA Index System (NDIS) is being developed to link databases in numerous states. A similar computer matching system, the National Integrated Ballistics Information Network (NIBIN), matches ballistics evidence in an attempt to link shooting incidents.

CODIS AT WORK

The facts could hardly be worse. September 21, 1993. Eastfield Community College in Mesquite. A young couple, married just eleven days, jogging on the track. A gunman confronted them. He demanded money. They told him they had none. He ordered them to lie down. They complied. Then the newlyweds prayed. The gunman demanded, "Where is your God now?" as he kicked Douglas White. He then fired two shots. They were fatal. The gunman forced Lori White into some nearby bushes. With a gun at her head, he raped her. She prayed throughout the assault. The gunman fled.

Seven and a half years later, Mesquite police were still unable to solve the crime. It wasn't for lack of effort. They investigated over 200 leads, compared DNA samples from 40 suspects. *America's Most Wanted* even featured the murder-rape on nationwide TV.

Then came the break. It was January, 2001. The state's new CODIS system compared the rapist's DNA, recovered from

Lori's medical exam shortly after the assault, with its database of known DNA samples. There was a match: Alvin Avon Braziel.

Braziel was in prison, finishing up a 5-year sentence for rape of a child. His release was scheduled for January 2002, but that release never came. Instead he was taken to Dallas County, tried, convicted, and sentenced to death. By August 9, 2001—eight long years after the murder but barely seven months after CODIS had done its job—Braziel was sitting in a cell on death row.

After they know who did it, the officers must review the facts to determine whether they have enough evidence to arrest the person. In some jurisdictions, the prosecutor's office helps review the case. Once officers decide to arrest, they must adhere to certain legal requirements.

AMERICA'S MOST HELPFUL

One of Texas' best crime fighting tools has been the national TV show *America's Most Wanted* (AMW). How helpful has it been? Consider the following:

Angel Maturino Resendiz. The Railroad Killer. Implicated in at least 13 murders. Caught due to a tip from an AMW viewer. He was convicted of a Houston doctor's rape/murder and sentenced to die. Today, he sits on death row.

Kenneth Allen McDuff. Serial killer. Suspected in at least 9 murders. Caught in Missouri due to a tip from an AMW viewer. He was convicted of two Central Texas murders and given the death penalty. He was executed on November 17, 1998.

Texas Seven. Seven inmates who escaped from a South Texas prison and embarked on a crime spree which included the murder of an Irving police officer. They were caught in Colorado due to a tip from an AMW viewer. All six inmates who were caught (the seventh committed suicide) were convicted of capital murder and sentenced to die. They are all sitting on death row.

In all, AMW has been responsible for over 800 arrests. That number grows weekly.

AMW is the brainchild of its host John Walsh. Walsh's interest in crime fighting came from his own personal tragedy when his 6 year old son Adam was abducted and killed in Florida in 1981. Since then, Walsh has been a tireless crusader

for missing children and victims' rights. But the success of AMW's crime fighting efforts, by taking hundreds of dangerous criminals off the streets, has saved thousands of families the same horror that he endured. In fact, the show could just as aptly be named *America's Most Helpful*.

ARREST An arrest occurs when a law enforcement officer takes a criminal suspect into custody. An arrest can be made either with or without a warrant.

ARREST WARRANTS An arrest warrant is very similar to a search warrant. In writing, a judge authorizes a law enforcement officer to place a suspect in custody for a specific offense. The judge bases an arrest warrant on a sworn statement. This written statement names the suspects or gives a reasonably specific description of them. It also explains the probable cause for why the officer making the statement believes the suspects have committed the crime.

Many technical rules apply, and law enforcement officers frequently ask someone from the prosecutor's office to help. In many instances, an investigation has produced probable cause to arrest the suspects, but the officers believe they will find more evidence or stolen property at the place where they arrest the suspects, and so they need to obtain a search warrant as well. In these cases, the judge can issue both a search warrant and an arrest warrant on the basis of a single sworn statement.

Although an arrest warrant must be in writing, the officers making the arrest do not have to see it. They can get the information from a computer or hear it broadcast on a police radio. On the basis of such information, any peace officer may arrest the suspects.

ARREST WITHOUT WARRANT It is not always practical or safe for an officer to wait until he or she can obtain a warrant before arresting a suspect. Texas law allows arrests without warrants when the officer

- sees suspects commit a crime
- finds suspects in a suspicious place under circumstances which reasonably show they are guilty of a crime
- has probable cause to believe the suspects have assaulted someone and may do so again, or that they have assaulted a family member
- has probable cause to believe the suspects have committed a felony and are about to escape

SWIFT JUSTICE

The general perception is that criminal trials are long, drawn-out proceedings. This, in part, is based upon trials which occur in other states and upon a few highly publicized national trials.

Most felony jury trials in Texas, even serious murder cases, are completed within one week. A few may extend into the following week. Month-long criminal trials are rare.

Consider the trial of Houston-area dentist Clara Harris. She was charged with murdering her orthodontist husband in a jealous rage after discovering him in a hotel with his mistress. The trial testimony established that Harris waited for her husband in the parking lot, ran over him three times, and then parked her Mercedes-Benz with one wheel on top of him.

It was one of the most highly publicized trials in Texas in the past decade. National and international media personnel descended on Houston.

The defendant was ably represented by a team of lawyers led by one of Harris County's most aggressive, experienced criminal defense lawyers. There was a steady procession of fact witnesses, character witnesses, and expert witnesses called by both sides. Even the mistress and the defendant testified. Yet, the entire trial lasted just 17 days. In fact, only 205 days elapsed from the murder on July 24, 2002, until Harris was locked up to begin her 20-year sentence on February 14, 2003.

JUDGE Within a few hours after suspects are arrested, an officer takes them to a judge in that county. In most counties this judge will be a justice of the peace or municipal judge. However, in some counties, including Harris, suspects are taken before a district judge.

The judge, citing a specific law, tells the accused why they were arrested. As with the Miranda warnings, the judge also tells the accused about their rights

- to hire a lawyer
- to remain silent
- to have a lawyer present during questioning
- to stop the questions at any time
- to get a free lawyer
- to have an examining trial

Finally, the judge sets bail.

BAIL Bail is an amount of money set by a judge that defendants must give to the court as security; defendants pay bail in order to be released from custody, on the condition that they will appear in court at a later date. If they are released and do not appear, a warrant will be issued for their arrest and the amount of the bond will be surrendered. Posting bail entitles defendants to release from jail as long as they appear for all of their court dates.

AMOUNT OF BAIL The amount of bail is usually set by the judge who first sees suspects after their arrest. If the suspects are later indicted for felonies, the district judge will review the bail and either change or approve the amount.

In setting bail, a judge follows a set of legal guidelines. As a general rule, a judge should

- set bail to ensure that the defendants will appear in court, but not so high that it functions as "an instrument of oppression"
- consider the defendants' ability to make bail (their financial resources)
- consider the defendants' ties to the community—family, friends, job, length of residence, and so on

Using these guidelines, the judge would set a low bail amount for defendants with few financial resources but strong community ties. These guidelines are still in effect, but the legislature added a new guideline: "The future safety of a victim of the alleged offense and the community shall be considered." Now, a judge should balance the defendant's right to bail against the victim's rights and the community's safety.

Sometimes a judge does not have to set bail; for instance, if the defendants are charged with capital murder or with multiple crimes. In these cases, the prosecutor must file a motion to deny bail. The prosecutor must also show the judge evidence that the defendants are guilty and, in a capital murder case, that they will probably receive death sentences.

TYPES OF BAIL When posting bail, defendants have three choices: surety bonds, cash bonds, and personal bonds. Professional bonding companies post surety bonds for a fee of usually 10% to 20% of the bail amount. Then they write a bond that obligates them to pay the county the entire sum if the defendants do not appear in court when scheduled. The bonding company's fees are not refundable to the defendants. In most of the larger counties, bonding companies are licensed and must have a certain percentage of the bail bonds that they write deposited as cash with the local bail bond board.

Anyone can make a cash bond by simply depositing the amount of bail with the clerk of the court. If defendants make all of their scheduled court appearances, these bonds are fully refundable after the cases are over. Sometimes a judge will approve a "percentage cash bond," which will allow defendants to post a percentage of the total amount of bail. Such a bond is refundable at the conclusion of a case.

With personal bonds, defendants are released without any security. Basically, they are released from custody on the basis of their promise to appear in court. Many counties have pretrial release offices that prepare reports for the judge about whether or not the defendants should get a personal bond. These offices charge a nonrefundable release fee of the greater of $20 or 3% of the bail amount.

CONDITIONS ON BOND The judge may grant bail but impose certain conditions, such as home confinement, electronic monitoring, and weekly drug testing. For personal bonds, the judge may also impose alcohol testing and may require drug or alcohol treatment or education programs.

In addition to these general conditions, the judge may also impose specific conditions for specific crimes. In a case involving a sexual offense against a child 12 years or under, the judge may require that defendants not communicate with victims and not go near the residence, school, or other locations which the victims frequent. The judge may place similar conditions on defendants charged with stalking.

FAMILY VIOLENCE Posting bail normally allows defendants to be released immediately, but defendants in family violence cases may be held up to 48 hours after bond is posted. The head of an agency (usually a police chief or sheriff) may order such defendants to be held for 4 additional hours. A written order from a judge can extend custody for up to 20 additional hours or, if the judge finds that the defendant likely committed family violence and has a prior arrest for family violence or certain other violent crimes, the judge can extend custody for 44 additional hours.

GRAND JURY A grand jury consists of 12 citizens of a county. They determine whether the prosecutors have sufficient evidence to justify a prosecution. If the grand jury says yes, it issues a true-bill in the form of an indictment. An indictment is a piece of paper, signed by the grand jury foreperson and filed in court, that charges a defendant with a specific crime. If the grand jury says no, it issues a no-bill, which dismisses the case.

Grand jurors are usually selected by way of a commissioner system. The district judge selects 3, 4, or 5 grand jury commissioners. These commissioners select up to 40 citizens of the county. The district judge then notifies them to appear. The first 12 who are qualified to serve make up the grand jury. In an alternative method, which is not widely used, the grand jurors are selected at random from the qualified citizens of the county. Grand jurors must

- be citizens of the state and county
- be qualified voters
- be of sound mind and good moral character
- be able to read and write
- not have been convicted of any felony
- not be under indictment or other legal accusation for theft or any felony

Grand jurors generally meet for terms of 2 to 6 months. Depending on the size of the county, grand jurors may meet only once or twice, or they may meet several times a week. The grand jurors meet in secret. The local felony prosecutor, acting as their lawyer, presents evidence by calling witnesses such as police officers, victims, and eyewitnesses. The prosecutor may also read witnesses' statements or crime lab reports. Defendants may appear before the grand jury. Any defense lawyers must wait outside the grand jury room. While the grand jurors discuss and vote on a case, the prosecutor may not be present, either.

The district judge appoints a foreperson of the grand jury who presides over the grand jury's work. Nine members of the grand jury must be present to conduct business. A true-bill requires at least 9 affirmative votes regardless of the number of grand jurors present.

At the end of each session, the grand jury notifies the judge or clerk of its actions. The prosecutor prepares written indictments, which the foreperson signs. The clerk then has the indictments delivered to the defendants. Those defendants who are no-billed are notified and, if necessary, released from jail.

PRETRIAL MATTERS After a grand jury returns an indictment, the defendants get a copy. In a few cases, the defendants have not been arrested and a judge issues a warrant for their arrest. After they are arrested, they get a copy of the indictment. Then the defendants get notice to appear in court. The exact procedure for and names given to this step vary widely from court to court. Generally, this stage is referred to as a "docket call" or "announcement docket." Sometimes this procedure is handled by telephone. At this time, the defendants must tell the court the names of their lawyers. If the defendants are indigent and have not already had lawyers appointed, a judge will appoint them at this stage.

DEFENSE LAWYERS Any of the more than 73,000 lawyers licensed to practice law in Texas may represent a criminal defendant. As a practical matter, criminal law is a specialty which only a portion of all lawyers handle. Larger counties have a group of lawyers who either handle criminal cases only or make criminal cases a major portion of their practice. In smaller counties, lawyers with more general practices may include criminal law.

Defendants hire defense lawyers, usually for a pre-negotiated flat fee ranging anywhere from a few hundred dollars to tens of thousands of dollars or more. The fee will depend on the seriousness of the crime, the reputation of the lawyer, and the resources of the defendant.

Indigent defendants are entitled to court-appointed defense lawyers who are paid by the local county as directed by the judge who appoints them. Court-appointed lawyer fees vary widely but are generally less, and in many cases substantially less, than the lawyer would normally charge.

Court-appointed lawyers are not second-rate lawyers. Although it is true that many young, inexperienced lawyers get their first courtroom experience this way, judges usually match the lawyer's level of experience to the complexity and severity of the case. Court-appointed lawyers come from the same pool of criminal lawyers from which nonindigent defendants hire their lawyers.

123,630 **times in 2003 attorneys were appointed to handle felony criminal cases.**

Source: Texas Judicial Council and Office of Court Administration

PSYCHIATRIC MATTERS The related questions of competency and sanity can be addressed by way of a psychiatric exam. Thus, the defense lawyer may ask the court to appoint a psychiatrist. If the facts indicate psychiatric problems, the judge will routinely grant these motions. The exam and the psychiatrist's report generally take several weeks.

Mental competency refers to defendants' state of mind at the time of their trials. Defendants must be mentally competent to stand trial. *Competency* means that they must have the mental ability to consult their lawyers with a reasonable degree of understanding, and that they must have both a rational and a factual understanding of the criminal justice process in the proceedings against them.

Sanity refers to the defendants' state of mind at the time they committed the crimes. *Insanity* means severe mental diseases or defects that cause defendants not to know that their criminal actions were wrong at the time they did them. Legal insanity is a defense in Texas.

Most of the time, psychiatric reports indicate that a defendant is competent and sane. A small percentage of the time, a report indicates otherwise. If a defendant is not competent, the report must also give an opinion: can the defendant regain competence to stand trial? Usually, drug therapy at a state hospital can restore competency. A court proceeding will commit the defendant to a state hospital. Within a few months, the defendant is generally restored to competency and returned to stand trial.

The insanity defense is discussed at greater length in Chapter 3. It is very rarely successful in Texas.

PRETRIAL MOTIONS Before the trial begins, the defense lawyer will file pretrial motions. The number and kind of motions are limited primarily by the defense lawyer's imagination. It is not unusual for the defense to file more than fifty pages of such motions.

Motions to Discover Evidence Normally, the defense lawyer will file a motion seeking to see all of the state's evidence. The state is required to show their physical evidence and certain other items to the defense. As a practical matter, most prosecutors will reach an agreement with the defense lawyer as to what items will be shown or shared. Many prosecutors have what they call an "open-file" policy; the defense can review all reports and witness statements prior to the trial.

The defense will also file a Brady motion. This motion received its name from a United States Supreme Court case called *Brady v Maryland*. The Supreme Court held that prosecutors must turn over to the defense any evidence which indicates that a defendant might not be guilty.

Prosecutors share evidence with defense lawyers or have open-file policies for two reasons. First, the prosecutors hope that when defense lawyers see the strength of the state's case, they will urge their clients to plead guilty. Second, such disclosure prevents convicted defendants from claiming years later that the prosecutors withheld Brady material.

The defense does not have to disclose its evidence to the state. Both the state and defense, if requested, must disclose a list of any expert witnesses that they wish to call at trial. This information must be provided 20 days before trial begins.

Motions to Suppress A motion to suppress gives a legal reason why the judge should not allow the prosecutor to use certain evidence at trial. The most common reason is that the evidence was found as a result of an illegal search and seizure. Such a motion usually requires police officers to testify and explain whatever facts justified their search for the evidence. Such motions are also used to challenge search warrants and arrest warrants.

Motions to suppress are frequently critical to the case. If the defense is successful, all or part of the prosecutor's evidence may not be allowed at trial. If the drugs in a drug prosecution are suppressed, for example, the judge will dismiss the case. In other cases, if only part of the evidence is excluded, the judge will not dismiss the case but the prosecutor's case may be greatly weakened. For example, if someone used an improperly written search warrant to obtain a murder weapon, the prosecutor may have to proceed without this important piece of evidence.

Using other suppression motions, lawyers can try to prevent the prosecutor from using a confession at trial. The judge listens to evidence about how the defendant confessed. These hearings are called "Jackson v Denno" hearings after the United States Supreme Court case which decided to require them. As with other motions to suppress, this pretrial hearing may be the most important part of the trial.

Motions Concerning Trial Procedures Several types of motions address how the trial will be conducted. Defendants must file a sworn application asking for probation (community supervision). They also file their choices as to whether they want the judge or the jury to set punishment.

The most publicized motion concerning trial procedures is the change of venue motion. This motion gives defendants a chance to prove that they cannot receive a fair trial in the county where the crime was committed. The most common reason for this motion is the amount of publicity the case has received.

GUILTY PLEAS Approximately 97% of criminal convictions in Texas are the results of guilty pleas. For most of these guilty pleas, a written plea agreement specifies what the defendant will plead guilty to and what punishment the prosecutor will recommend.

GUILTY-PLEA PROCEDURE Before accepting guilty pleas, judges must tell defendants the crimes they are charged with and the range of punishment for each. Judges must also warn all defendants that if they are not citizens of the United States, guilty pleas could have negative immigration consequences. Throughout the guilty-plea process, judges must determine that defendants are mentally competent and are making their guilty pleas freely and voluntarily.

During this process, judges will also ask whether a plea-bargaining agreement exists. If so, judges must tell defendants whether or not they will accept an agreement. If a judge will not, the defendant is entitled to withdraw the guilty plea.

In a felony case, the evidence must support the guilty plea. This is usually done by way of a written confession that sets out the facts that the prosecutors would prove at a trial. The defendant must agree that these facts are true.

Before finally accepting guilty pleas, judges will ask the prosecutors for a victim impact statement. For an extensive discussion of victim impact statements, see Chapter 5.

Before sentencing defendants, trial judges frequently request presentence reports. These reports, written by the probation department, describe the offense and the defendants' history as well as assess their rehabilitation needs. The reports also contain information about the impact of the crime on the victim.

Guilty-plea procedures vary widely across courts. In many courts, the required warnings, plea bargain agreement, and stipulation of evidence are written and signed by the lawyers and defendants before the judge comes to the courtroom. Very little may actually be said in court at the time of the guilty plea. In other courts, judges may spend time going over each step of the process with defendants.

PLEA BARGAINING Plea bargaining can take one of several forms:

1. Sentence bargaining—Defendants plead guilty in exchange for specific sentences, for example, 10 years in prison.

2. Charge bargaining—Defendants plead guilty to lesser offenses or to fewer offenses than are actually charged. For example, they plead guilty to two of three burglaries.

3. Parole eligibility bargaining—Defendants plead guilty only to charges that make them eligible for parole sooner. Or they do not plead guilty to a deadly weapon finding, which makes them eligible for parole much sooner.

4. Agreements not to file additional charges—Defendants may have committed multiple crimes. The prosecutor who wants to focus only on the most serious crimes or a representative sample of crimes may agree not to file other charges.

These plea bargains are not mutually exclusive and are frequently mixed. In a typical plea bargain, the defendant enters a plea of guilty to one of the charges in the indictment and the prosecutor recommends a certain sentence.

For victims, a plea bargain has several advantages. It eliminates a trial jury with a possible not-guilty verdict. The outcome is certain. The criminals are convicted. They are sentenced. Also, the victims avoid the time and emotional drain of a jury trial. A guilty plea takes a few minutes compared to a week or more for a trial. Finally, a guilty plea eliminates the appeal process, which may result in an appeals court ordering a new trial several years after the original trial.

Critics often cite secrecy and leniency as disadvantages of a plea bargain. Secrecy is not the problem it was a few years ago. Victims of serious crimes are usually informed of plea agreements, and judges frequently want to know the victims' thoughts about the plea agreement. The agreement itself must be in writing and is a public record. Leniency varies from case to case. Undoubtedly, overly lenient plea agreements do exist. However, most plea agreements are based upon an assessment of the actual sentence a judge or jury would impose on a particular defendant. Many plea agreements call for very substantial prison sentences.

JURY SELECTION The very few cases not resolved by guilty pleas are set for trial. Both the state and the defendant have the right to a jury to decide guilt. Only the defendant decides whether a judge or a jury sets punishment. A defendant who pleads guilty may have a jury only to set punishment.

A jury trial begins when citizens are summoned by mail to come to the courthouse, usually on a Monday morning. The list of prospective jurors is taken from the pool of citizens who have been issued driver's licenses or who are registered voters.

Jurors must

- be qualified (but not necessarily registered) to vote
- not have been convicted of theft or any felony
- not currently be legally accused of theft or any felony
- be literate and sane
- not have any physical disability that would interfere with jury duty
- not have prior involvement with the case, such as being a witness or a grand juror who heard the case

Otherwise-qualified jurors may also claim exemptions from jury service. These exemptions are optional, and the potential jurors may wish to serve without claiming the exemption. The main exemptions are age (over 70) and having children under 10 for whom the juror provides care.

Felony juries have 12 members; misdemeanor juries have 6. Judges may allow selection of up to 4 alternate jurors in a felony case and 2 in a misdemeanor case. Alternate jurors hear evidence and take the place of regular jurors who become disabled during trial. After juries begin deliberation (the guilt phase of the trial), judges dismiss unused alternate jurors. As a practical matter, alternate jurors are used only on capital murder cases or other exceptionally long cases.

After judges establish the jurors' basic qualifications, they allow both prosecutors and defense lawyers to talk to the potential jurors and ask them questions. This process of jury selection is called "voir dire." The term *voir dire* derives from French and basically means "to speak the truth."

During questioning, lawyers may ask judges to disqualify any juror for cause. Lawyers might believe that a juror would not be fair for some reason or unable to follow part of the law that is applicable to the case. The lawyers ask questions to determine whether the potential jurors can follow the law, what they know about the case on trial, and their backgrounds and attitudes.

After both sides have talked to the potential jurors, they must make their peremptory challenges. Both sides can make peremptory challenges without giving a reason for the challenge. Other than for the reasons of race or gender, the lawyers may strike equal numbers of any potential jurors—10 for a non–death penalty felony and 3 for most misdemeanors.

The peremptory challenges are made on a list which each side must turn in separately to the clerk. The clerk then determines the first 12 (or 6) potential jurors who were not removed for cause or struck with a peremptory challenge. These potential jurors are then called to sit in the jury box and they become the jury in the case.

TRIAL PROCEDURE

COURTROOM PERSONNEL After the jury is selected, the trial can begin. While every trial has unique facts and personalities, the courtroom personnel and the structure of the trial are constant:

- The judge presides over the trial, sets the hours of the trial, moves the trial through its various stages, and decides legal matters that come up during the trial.
- The bailiff shepherds the jury into and out of the courtroom. The bailiff also escorts witnesses to the witness stand, an-

nounces the court into session, and generally maintains order in the courtroom.

• The court reporter makes a record of all the words spoken by the participants during the trial. The court reporter marks and preserves the various "exhibits" (physical items offered into evidence such as photographs, weapons, etc.).

• The clerk keeps up the official court file of the case. The clerk usually administers the oath to the witnesses.

• The court administrator schedules cases for courtroom time and will be present in the courtroom from time to time.

• The prosecutor represents the State of Texas.

• The defense lawyer represents the defendant.

• The defendant must be present in the courtroom, although judges can exclude disruptive defendants.

WITNESSES The witnesses are not usually allowed in the courtroom unless both lawyers agree. Under the Rule of Witnesses, which is often called simply The Rule, a witness is not permitted in the courtroom while other witnesses are testifying. The Rule is designed to keep witnesses from changing their testimony based upon what other witnesses say. As a result, the victim, if a witness, often has to stay out of the courtroom during the trial. The trial judge can exempt the victim from The Rule. (See Chapter 5.)

STRUCTURE OF THE TRIAL

Guilt Phase The trial begins when the judge instructs the prosecutor to read the charges—an indictment in a felony case or an information in a misdemeanor case. The defendant enters a plea of "guilty" or "not guilty" in front of the jury. The judge then gives the prosecution an opportunity to make an opening statement. Such a statement summarizes what facts the state expects to prove and how it will prove them. The defense also has a chance to make an opening statement, although it may reserve this opportunity until later in the case.

The State's Case After opening statements, the prosecutor begins to call witnesses. Each witness called is first questioned by the prosecutor (direct examination). Then the defense lawyer may question the witness (cross-examination). This questioning can continue back and forth until both sides are finished.

The prosecutor will also have the witnesses identify the exhibits and answer questions about them. The court reporter will use a sticker to mark the exhibits for ease of identification. The sticker will indicate "State's Exhibit No. ____" with sequential numbers to distinguish the exhibits. Later, if the defense has exhibits, the court reporter will mark them "Defense Exhibit No. ____."

Before showing an exhibit to the jurors, the lawyer who wants to show it must question the witness about it. This questioning must establish facts indicating that the exhibit is accurate or genuine. These questions are called the "predicate for the exhibit."

When the lawyer feels that the predicate has been established, he or she will show the exhibit to the other lawyer and ask the judge to admit the exhibit into evidence. The other lawyer can either object or not. Most objections to exhibits involve the claim that the legal predicate has not been established or that the evidence was illegally obtained.

After hearing both lawyers, the judge will either admit or not admit the exhibit into evidence. If it is admitted, the witness or the lawyer can show it to the jury. After the state has called all of its witnesses, the state rests.

The Defendant's Case The defense lawyer then has an opportunity to make an opening statement if he or she has not already done so. The defense is not required to put on any evidence, but may do so. If it chooses to put on evidence, it calls witnesses and offers exhibits in the same manner as the prosecution did. At the conclusion of its case, the defense also rests.

Rebuttal If the defense puts on evidence, the state has an opportunity to call witnesses for rebuttal. The defense has an opportunity then to call any additional witnesses to rebut this testimony. This process very seldom goes beyond a few additional witnesses. After each side is done with rebuttal, it closes its case.

Jury Charge When both sides close, the judge reads the jury's instructions aloud. This jury charge

- summarizes the law applicable to the case
- explains what issue the jury needs to decide
- instructs the jury on how to deliberate
- contains verdict forms for the jury's decision

Normally, the judge asks the jury to reach a verdict of guilty or not guilty on one or more charges. The judge may also ask the jury to find a specific fact. For example, was a deadly weapon used or exhibited during the crime?

Final Arguments The lawyers make their final arguments in this order: prosecution, defense, prosecution.

Verdict After arguments, the bailiff hands the written charge to the jury. The bailiff escorts the jury members to the jury room, where they select a foreperson and begin their deliberations. They are kept together until they make a decision. With the consent of both the prosecution and defense, the trial judge may allow them to separate at night to go home and sleep.

In a Texas criminal case, the jury's decision or verdict must be unanimous. In relatively few cases, the jury is unable to reach a unanimous verdict. This is called a "hung jury." The judge must declare a mistrial, and the trial will have to return to the jury selection phase. These are the other possible outcomes:

- If the jury finds the defendant not guilty on all charges, the trial is over.
- If the jury finds the defendant guilty of one or more charges, either the judge or jury, according to the defendant's previous decision, will set punishment.
- If the judge is setting punishment, the judge will dismiss the jury. He can then hear evidence and set the punishment immediately or delay sentencing until a later time.
- If the jury is setting punishment, the judge will immediately begin the punishment phase of the trial.

Punishment Phase The punishment phase of the trial is almost identical to the guilt phase. The prosecution reads any penalty paragraphs contained in the indictment. These paragraphs list prior prison sentences of the defendant and increase the possible punishment. If there are penalty paragraphs, the defendant will plead "true" or "not true" to each prior prison sentence.

After opening statements, the lawyers call witnesses and offer evidence, as they did during the guilt phase. During the guilt phase of the trial, the prosecution is not allowed to offer evidence of prior convictions or other crimes committed by the defendant. During the punishment phase, these prior convictions or crimes can be presented to the jury.

The defense offers evidence to mitigate or lessen punishment. Such evidence usually includes testimony from the defendant's mother, other relatives and friends, employers, and possibly an expert witness such as a probation officer or psychiatrist.

Punishment Verdict After both sides rest and close, the trial judge again prepares a written jury charge. The judge reads the charge to the jury, the lawyers make final arguments, and the jury deliberates until it reaches a verdict on punishment. This verdict will include the length of confinement and the amount of any fine. If the defendant is legally eligible, and the confinement is 10 years or fewer, the jury can suspend the sentence and place the defendant on probation. The judge will set the exact length of such a probation.

LEGAL CONCEPTS AT TRIAL There are certain basic legal concepts which are central to the ways trials are conducted. These concepts require the prosecution to prove guilt and ensure defendants' protection against self-incrimination. All defendants are entitled to the presumption of innocence. That is, defendants do not have to prove that they are innocent; rather, the prosecutor must prove that they are guilty. Another key legal concept is the burden of proof. The burden of proof is on the state, which means that the prosecutor must come forward with evidence that proves defendants are guilty.

Most lawsuits are tried using a standard called a "preponderance of evidence." This standard requires that one side of the lawsuit must probably be right—sort of a 51% requirement. A higher standard, clear and convincing evidence, is used in some lawsuits. The highest standard, proof beyond a reasonable doubt, is reserved for criminal cases. It applies to all criminal cases from the least serious traffic offense to the most heinous violent act.

Proof beyond a reasonable doubt applies only to the elements of the offense such as the identity of the defendant and the necessary facts that make up the crime. Other facts—such as the exact time of day, the type of clothes worn, and why the crime was committed—do not have to be proved.

Defendants have an absolute right not to testify in a criminal case. Whether or not to testify is a personal choice that defendants must make after consulting with their lawyers. Defendants who choose to testify, like any other witnesses, are subject to cross-examination.

In deciding whether or not to testify, defendants must think about how their prior criminal history will sound to a jury. Generally, a jury does not learn about prior convictions until the punishment phase of the trial. However, if defendants testify during the guilt phase, the prosecutor can question them, within certain limits. For example, the prosecutor can ask about prior felony convictions and about misdemeanor convictions, such as theft, that involve moral turpitude. The answers to these questions may, in the jurors' minds, reflect negatively on a defendant's character.

Bifurcated trial simply means a two-part trial. The two phases—the guilt phase and the punishment phase—help ensure that defendants are tried solely for their guilt on one particular crime. Until the punishment phase, all of the evidence about prior criminal history or other bad acts or crimes they have committed cannot be admitted as evidence against them.

RULES OF EVIDENCE The Texas Rules of Criminal Evidence are a set of written rules that instruct trial judges as to what evidence is properly heard by the fact finder—either the judge or jury. These rules are based on the Federal Rules of Evidence, which the federal courts and many states follow. The rules are approved by the Texas Court of Criminal Appeals. The Texas Rules of Criminal Evidence are divided into 11 articles. Each article covers several rules.

One article states that all evidence must be relevant. This means the evidence must have a tendency to prove that some fact important to the lawsuit is more probably true or less probably true because of the evidence. Relevant evidence, however, may not be admissible if it might unfairly prejudice a jury. The judge must balance relevance and unfair prejudice in deciding whether to allow certain evidence to be heard. For example, a defendant named John is charged with burglary. It might be relevant that John was familiar with the neighborhood because he worked across the street from the burglarized home. The fact that the place where John worked was a pornographic book store would be prejudicial. Before admitting the evidence, the judge would have to balance the answers to two questions: How relevant is John's familiarity with the area? How much will the jury be prejudiced by knowledge of John's unsavory employment? Defense lawyers often make objections based upon relevance or unfair prejudice.

Another common objection concerns hearsay. Witnesses can testify only about what they saw or heard. They cannot testify about what Joan, for example, told them that she saw or heard. That's hearsay. However, statements Joan made during the crime to a victim or witness are not hearsay.

Hearsay can be admitted into evidence under certain special circumstances. Texas law allows 24 such exceptions. One, an excited utterance, is a statement about a startling event made when the speaker was still under the influence of the event. Tape-recorded phone calls to 911 by crime victims are frequently allowed into evidence as excited utterances.

The Rules of Evidence also provide for certain privileges. That is, some people have the right or duty not to testify about certain subjects.

- The lawyer-client privilege requires lawyers not to tell what their clients have told them.
- The husband-wife privilege requires spouses not to testify against each other. This privilege does not apply when the victim

of the crime is the person's spouse, a minor child, or a member of either spouse's household.

- Another privilege protects information given to members of the clergy in their professional capacity.
- There is no physician-patient privilege in Texas.

Other articles in the Rules of Evidence cover opinion testimony, evidence about prior convictions, expert witnesses, government and business records, photographs, and writings. These rules apply to all criminal cases. However, they do not apply to grand jury proceedings, search and arrest warrants, and certain bail proceedings.

APPEAL Convicted defendants have a right to have another court review their trial to determine whether it was fair and followed proper procedures. This review is called an "appeal." An appeal of a conviction for a minor crime where the original trial was in justice of the peace court or municipal court is called a *trial de novo*, or new trial. This type of appeal requires that the case be tried over from the beginning in the county court.

An appeal from most misdemeanors and all felonies is based upon a review of the record. A panel of three judges on one of the 14 courts of appeals reviews it. These judges can affirm (leave alone) or reverse the conviction (that is, order a new trial before the original court). One of the judges writes an opinion explaining the reasons.

If either side is dissatisfied with the appeal court's decision, the lawyers for that side can file a Petition for Discretionary Review (PDR) with the Texas Court of Criminal Appeals. The Court of Criminal Appeals usually refuses to hear the case. However, in a small percentage of cases, it reviews and sometimes changes the lower appeals court's decision. If either side wishes to have the case heard further, the only appeal left is to the United States Supreme Court, which seldom hears a noncapital criminal case.

In reviewing a conviction on appeal, the court is limited to looking at the record from the trial. The record consists of the papers filed in court, the exhibits at trial, and a verbatim transcript of every word spoken during the trial.

An appeal begins when the defendant gives notice of appeal; that is, written notice that the defendant wants his or her case reviewed. The record is then prepared. This process takes several months. After the record is complete, the defense has 30 days to file a written list of complaints about the trial together with the legal arguments about why these complaints are valid. This document is called a "brief." The prosecution then has 25 days to file a written answer to the defense arguments. This document is also called a brief. The time limits for either side can be extended by the appeals court. Normally, this process takes four to six months.

After the briefs are filed, the court of appeals will review the case. If the lawyers request, the court will schedule the case for a formal oral presentation by both sides. This hearing, known as "oral arguments," is limited to 20 to 30 minutes for each side. The judges can question both sides during the oral arguments. After that, the judges will spend weeks or months making a decision and writing the opinion.

After the appeals are decided and time limits for further appeals have elapsed, convictions become final. The appeals court issues a written mandate which ends the criminal process. Mandates order that sentences be carried out. If defendants are not already in custody serving their sentences, an arrest warrant will be issued and, after arrest, they will begin to serve their sentences.

DEATH PENALTY The trial of a death penalty case, or capital murder, as it is formally known, follows the same procedure as any other criminal case, with three broad exceptions.

JURY SELECTION In a death penalty case, both sides individually question each prospective juror. This process is known as "individual voir dire." In addition to the normal questions lawyers ask prospective jurors, both sides will question jurors about their attitude toward the death penalty. Jurors can be excused if they are opposed to the death penalty and could not, regardless of the evidence, vote for a verdict which would result in the death penalty. This individual questioning greatly lengthens the jury selection process. Whereas juries can normally be picked in two to three hours, death penalty juries frequently take up to three weeks.

The process of making peremptory challenges is also different in a death penalty case. As each potential juror is questioned, the judge rules on any challenges for cause. If the potential juror is not successfully challenged for cause, the prosecutor can excuse the juror with a peremptory challenge. If the prosecutor accepts the juror, the defense lawyer gets the same opportunity to accept or excuse the juror. If both sides accept the juror, he or she becomes part of the jury. Each side is allowed 15 peremptory challenges.

PUNISHMENT PHASE In a capital murder case, only 2 punishments are possible: life in prison or death by lethal injection. Unlike the punishment phase of other criminal trials, the jury does not decide on one of these two options. Instead, the jury answers certain questions about mitigating circumstances and about how dangerous the defendant might be in the future. On the basis of these answers, the judge sentences the defendant to either life in prison or death.

APPEAL If life imprisonment is the punishment, the appeal process is exactly the same as for any other criminal case. However, if death is the punishment, an appeal is automatic. It goes directly to the Court of Criminal Appeals.

CHRONOLOGY OF AN EXECUTION

Citizens are bewildered and upset at the lengthy appeal process afforded death row inmates. The process is long and complex because an inmate who fully appeals a death sentence will have the conviction reviewed by a minimum of 4 courts and 22 different judges in both the state and federal systems. During this lengthy review, further delays grow from new rounds of reviews based upon laws or court decisions which occurred after the original trial. Following is the chronology of a capital case from crime to execution.

The crime involved Carl Eugene Kelly and a codefendant robbing a Waco 7-Eleven clerk at gunpoint. The robbers abducted both the clerk and his friend and later shot both of them in the head at close range. They then dumped the bodies over a cliff. Kelly had prior convictions for theft and robbery.

September 2, 1980	**Murders occur; Kelly arrested**
October 23, 1980	**Grand jury indicts Kelly for capital murder**
June 4, 1981	**Jury convicts Kelly of capital murder**
June 5, 1981	**Jury sentences Kelly to death**
April 25, 1984	**Court of Criminal Appeals upholds conviction and death sentence**
October 29, 1984	**United States Supreme Court refuses to hear appeal**
December 14, 1984	**Trial judge sets execution date for February 21, 1985**
February 15, 1985	**Court of Criminal Appeals rejects Kelly's habeas corpus writ and denies stay of execution**
February 19, 1985	**United States District Court stays execution to consider Kelly's habeas corpus writ**
July 8, 1987	**United States District Court denies Kelly's habeas corpus writ; Kelly appeals this decision**

December 22, 1988	United States Court of Appeals denies Kelly's appeal
July 3, 1989	United States Supreme Court again declines to hear Kelly's appeal
January 5, 1990	Trial judge sets second execution date for February 21, 1990
February 16, 1990	Kelly files new habeas corpus claim saying he is entitled to a new trial based upon a 1989 Supreme Court decision in the *Penry* case
February 21, 1990	Court of Criminal Appeals grants stay of execution to consider new claim
February 19, 1992	Court of Criminal Appeals denies new claim
May 20, 1992	Trial court schedules third execution date for July 31, 1992
July 29, 1992	United States Supreme Court grants stay of execution
June 28, 1993	United States Supreme Court decides several Texas cases and, based on those decisions, again declines to hear a new appeal from Kelly
July 1, 1993	Trial judge sets a fourth execution date of August 20, 1993
August 16, 1993	Kelly files new appeal with original trial court
August 17, 1993	Trial court rejects appeal
August 18, 1993	Court of Criminal Appeals denies appeal
August 19, 1993	United States Supreme Court declines to block execution
August 20, 1993	Kelly is executed

A total of 12 years and 76 days elapsed between Kelly's sentencing and execution for the robbery, kidnapping, and murder of Steven Pryor.

In order to reduce this length of time from trial to execution, a number of procedures to streamline the process were put into place in the mid-1990s. A death row inmate can still have his case reviewed by 22 judges at 4 different levels but under the new procedures some of the appeals are done

simultaneously. The new procedures seem to be working. Of the 24 inmates executed in 2003, four were executed within 6 years of their crime and the overall average was barely 10 years.

The first chapter laid the foundation for the system by discussing the personnel that make up the justice system and sketching the court system. In this chapter, I added the framework by showing the operation of the system from investigation through the final appeal. Now it is time to turn to the actual crimes—their definitions and punishment ranges. We will begin with an actual crime, the very real story of a con artist whose operating methods earned him the name "The Love Bandit."

CHAPTER 3

CRIMINAL LAW

The story of the Love Bandit reads like fiction, but it is very true.

The Love Bandit used a string of aliases such as Mark Lanson, Randy Fox, and Randy Fuchs. Posing as a Harvard-educated lawyer, he practiced his trade of professional conning. But unlike other con artists, who are usually satisfied by appealing to their victims' greed, the Love Bandit went straight to their hearts. He met middle-aged single women, romanced and wooed them, met their children and family, and proposed marriage. While getting their finances in order for their future life together, the Love Bandit stole their life's savings and vanished without a trace.

Even for a con artist, using love and marriage as a weapon was a new level of cruelty. One of his victims had already picked out her wedding dress. To have your money stolen would be awful enough. To then realize that all the romance—the roses, the wine, the "I love you's"—was a calculated lie, would be devastating.

During the late 1980s and early 1990s, the Love Bandit struck four times in Central Texas. His mistake was selecting a victim in Round Rock who reported the crime. It was assigned to police department investigator Ed Nendell. Nendell became incensed at the tactics the Love Bandit had used and became obsessed with tracking him down.

Nendell tracked the Love Bandit through Kansas, New Mexico, Oklahoma, and Arizona. He was never able to learn his true identity and never able to catch up with him. But Nendell was not going to give up. He relentlessly pursued every lead and was even featured in a cover story in *Redbook* magazine.

The break in the case came on August 1, 1992, in Tempe, Arizona. The FBI was questioning a suspect about a false passport. One of the FBI agents, who had read the *Redbook* article, started to connect the two cases. An exchange of photographs quickly confirmed that the suspect in Tempe was in fact Nendell's Love Bandit.

Back in Texas to face trial, the Love Bandit claimed amnesia. He insisted he didn't know his real name and had no recollection of ever meeting the victims. In court, he always signed his name simply as "X."

The Love Bandit's courtroom con might have worked but for Nendell. All of his tenacious work came to the attention of ABC News in New York. A producer from *20/20* brought Tom Jarrell to Georgetown. He interviewed me as the Bandit's prosecutor and, of course, Ed Nendell, by then an investigator for my office.

The *20/20* story aired on the evening of January 22, 1993. On the show, I made a plea for anyone who could help identify the Love Bandit to contact my office or the Round Rock Police Department.

I watched *20/20* at home that night. The Love Bandit segment was second and finished around 9:40 A.M. At 10:15 my home phone rang. I answered.

A woman's voice asked, "Is this the Ken Anderson who is the district attorney?"

"Yes," I answered slowly.

"Are you the one who was just on *20/20*?"

"Yes," I answered, somewhat suspicious.

"Well, I know who the Love Bandit is. I'm his real wife. I'm living in Boston . . ."

Every prosecutor instinct I had told me that hers was a crank call. But she kept giving me details and they kept checking out. It took a couple more days to confirm everything, but we soon had the story.

The Love Bandit was Marion Ducote, a fugitive from Louisiana. He skipped town after bilking numerous would-be investors with a fraudulent oil investment scheme. He took his wife with him. However, after 30 days on the run, she abandoned him and returned home. Since Ducote was never arrested on the Louisiana charges, he had never been fingerprinted—something that had frustrated our efforts to identify him.

Ducote was ultimately convicted on our charges and sentenced to 10 years in prison. He later was convicted of 22 additional felonies—2 in federal court, 1 in Travis County, and 19 in Louisiana. He ultimately served 7½ years behind bars and remains on parole.

The story of the Love Bandit is a case of truth being stranger than fiction. It involves very real pain, financial and emotional, for his victims. It involves a hero, the tenacious investigator Ed Nendell. It involves drama, the nationwide search, the FBI agent who read a *Redbook* magazine, and the luck that Ducote's wife was watching *20/20* that evening. It is the kind of story that makes crime interesting.

As I often explain to juries, the legal definition is simply the skeleton of a crime. The actual facts—the victim, the defendant, the methods used in the crime, and the investigation—are the flesh and blood of our system, the truly interesting parts of criminal law.

But all crimes are not the same. Some of the punishment ranges will surprise you. The legislature has made clear judgments about the relative seriousness of various crimes. Some are low-level misdemeanors; some are serious felonies.

The legislature has toughened the penalties for violent offenders, for drunk drivers, and for child molesters. Those changes were long overdue. But the legislature also significantly lowered the penalties for neighborhood crack dealers. Frankly, I was surprised at how little public controversy arose when the penalty for street corner crack dealers fell. It used to be a first-degree felony—carrying a possible life sentence. It is now a state jail felony. In the long run, I'm convinced that this decision will be viewed as a serious mistake.

For better or worse, these judgments are made by real people—the state representatives and senators whom we elect. The next time you contact such officials, you may want to fuss at them. Or you may compliment them and be thankful that they, and not you, had to make these judgments. Regardless of your viewpoint, this chapter will give you the information you need in order to know exactly what decisions have been made for us.

THE LAWS Our criminal laws define crimes, specify the punishment for each crime, and stipulate the available defenses for each crime. Criminal laws are passed by the Texas legislature subject to the approval of the governor. The legislature meets during odd-numbered years. Usually, the lawmakers add new crimes or increase the punishment for existing crimes based upon current trends, such as drive-by shootings or increased gang activity.

You'll find criminal laws in four places:

- The Texas Penal Code defines the vast majority of crimes. It also indicates the basic punishment structure and defines most defenses, such as insanity and self-defense.
- The Controlled Substances Act, part of the Texas Health and Safety Code, contains all drug laws.

• Minor criminal violations of specific regulations dot other Texas laws. Some, such as traffic and game laws, are voluminous and very detailed.

• Local city ordinances define minor offenses which can be punished by a fine only.

TILTING AT WINDMILLS

It may seem an imposing task to change the laws of the State of Texas. What can an individual crime victim do? Here's the story of one mother who confronted a specific injustice in the system.

A brutal murder of a child is a parent's worst nightmare. Can you imagine the horror a mother must feel as she watches her daughter's killer being tried without the jury knowing that the killer had confessed?

That was exactly the horror Judy Brumelow felt as she sat in a Kerr County courtroom watching the brutal killer of her daughter tried on circumstantial evidence. Even though the killer had made a verbal confession to the crime, the jury was not allowed to hear about it. Why? Because the law did not let verbal confessions made by juveniles be offered as evidence at their trials.

Fortunately, the jury thought the circumstantial evidence was sufficient and convicted the killer. Judy, however, decided that no other mother should ever experience the outrage she experienced. She contacted her state representative, Parker McCollough. McCollough drafted legislation to correct the problem. In April 1991, Judy testified before a House committee. Two months later, in June, Governor Ann Richards signed into law the legislation authorizing verbal confessions by juveniles to be used at their trials.

Judy's experience wasn't unique. In the case of criminal law, the best lobbyists aren't the ones with fancy suits, big expense accounts, and plenty of campaign contributions. Rather, they are ordinary citizens who come forward with a specific injustice. If their cause is just, their story compelling, and they do their homework, their bill actually has a decent chance to pass.

PENAL CODE The Texas Penal Code breaks crimes into offenses against

- the person (e.g., murder, sexual assault)
- property (e.g., robbery, burglary, theft)
- public administration (e.g., bribery, perjury)
- public order and decency (e.g., riot, prostitution)
- public health, safety, and morals (e.g., DWI, unlawfully carrying a weapon)

CONTROLLED SUBSTANCES ACT The Controlled Substances Act defines all drug crimes. It also classifies hundreds of drugs as controlled substances and divides them into one of four penalty groups. The most serious penalty group includes heroin, cocaine, LSD, and methamphetamine.

The Controlled Substances Act lists four basic crimes:

- delivery of a controlled substance
- possession of a controlled substance
- delivery of marijuana
- possession of marijuana

Delivery means manufacturing the drugs, selling the drugs, or possessing the drugs with intent to sell. The punishment under each of these four groups is based upon the amount of the drug involved and the penalty group of the drug.

OTHER LAWS Many criminal laws are contained in specific regulations, such as the Traffic Code and the Fish and Game Code. While these are criminal violations, they are extremely minor and usually involve payment of only a small fine.

However, sometimes important criminal laws are mixed in with these regulations. For example, the Traffic Code has a law for Failure to Stop and Render Aid. This law is frequently used when drivers flee an injury collision and are found too late to prove intoxication. Under Failure to Stop and Render Aid, they can be prosecuted for a felony with confinement in prison for up to 5 years and a fine of up to $5,000.

CITY ORDINANCES Local city governments pass numerous regulations which are enforced through criminal sanctions. These ordinances involve parking, leash laws, allowing rubbish to accumulate, lawn watering, and a host of similar items. These offenses are punished with fines only and are prosecuted in municipal courts.

GENERAL PROVISIONS There are a few broad legal concepts that apply generally to all criminal definitions. The general provisions include the defendant's mental state, the law of parties, corporate responsibility, and age.

MENTAL STATE To commit a crime, a person must voluntarily either commit a proscribed act or possess an illegal object or substance. Purely accidental conduct is seldom a crime. A very few crimes, notably DWI and most traffic offenses, are strict liability offenses. That is, these crimes do not require any proof that the defendant acted voluntarily.

Four types of mental states characterize a crime in Texas. It must be

- intentional
- knowing
- reckless
- negligent

An intentional defendant acted on purpose, that is, with a conscious desire to engage in the crime. A knowing defendant acted with an awareness that the action caused the crime. The vast majority of criminals act both intentionally (on purpose) and knowingly (aware).

Two mental states—recklessness and criminal negligence—are less clear-cut. Reckless defendants act with an awareness that the action was likely to cause a crime, but they ignore that risk. Criminally negligent defendants act without awareness that the action was likely to cause a crime, but they do so under circumstances in which they should have been aware of the likelihood.

An example of recklessness: John Smith shoots a gun at a house without knowing whether anyone is inside. If someone is inside and is killed, John could be convicted of manslaughter (recklessly causing another person's death) even though he had no intent to kill anyone or knowledge that his action would kill anyone.

An example of criminal negligence: Mary Jones drives a car 25 miles per hour over the speed limit in a residential neighborhood. If a child darts out in front of the car and is killed, Mary could be found guilty of the crime of criminally negligent homicide (causing another person's death by criminal negligence). Even though you might refer to this incident as an accident, it would fit the definition of criminal negligence. Mary acted without awareness of the risk (that a child might dart out in front of the car) when she should have been aware of it.

PARTIES On TV and in most popular writing, an accomplice is a person who helps commit a crime. Texas law refers to such a person as a "party to the crime." A party aids or encourages someone else to commit the crime. A party is equally guilty of any crime he or she helps someone else commit. For example, Joe Carter, the wheel man in an armed robbery, may drive the car and serve as a lookout for another criminal who actually carries the gun into the store and robs the clerk. Joe is equally guilty of the robbery even though he didn't possess the gun, take the money, or even enter the store.

Some states make it a crime to help conceal or fail to report someone else's crime if you know about it. These laws are referred to by many names, including "accomplice after the fact" and "misprision of a felony." Traditionally, Texas had no such laws. However, the legislature has now made it a crime to fail to report child abuse (Class B misdemeanor) and to fail to report a felony involving death or serious bodily injury (Class A misdemeanor).

CORPORATIONS AND ASSOCIATIONS Normally, only individuals commit criminal offenses. However, sometimes a corporation or association can, and if convicted, it pays a fine. A *corporation* is a business organized under state laws. An *association* is any group of two or more people having a joint or common economic interest. For a corporation, someone in upper management must either authorize or recklessly tolerate the crime. The person who actually commits the crime can also be prosecuted.

AGE Most criminal laws apply only to people who are 17 years of age or older. Those between 10 and 16 enter the juvenile system. For prosecution of the most serious offenses, 14-, 15-, and 16-year-olds may transfer to the adult criminal system. Regardless of the accused person's age, the adult criminal system always tries certain crimes:

- perjury (if the accused had sufficient mental ability to understand the oath)
- traffic offenses
- fineable-only misdemeanors (e.g., minor in possession of alcohol)
- city ordinance violations (e.g., parking violations, leash law violations)

PUNISHMENTS All crimes are either felonies or misdemeanors. The five felony categories have a maximum possible sentence of either death or confinement in a state prison or state jail. Fines are optional. The three misdemeanor categories carry a maximum possible sentence of a year's confinement in a county jail, a fine, or both. These are the types of punishments for felonies:

- Capital felony: either life in prison or death by lethal injection. Capital murder is the only capital felony.
- First-degree felony: 5 to 99 years or life in prison. An optional fine of up to $10,000.
- Second-degree felony: 2 to 20 years in prison. An optional fine of up to $10,000.
- Third-degree felony: 2 to 10 years in prison. An optional fine of up to $10,000.
- State jail felony: 180 days to 2 years in a state jail. An optional fine of up to $10,000.

These are the types of punishments for misdemeanors:

- Class A misdemeanor: confinement not to exceed 1 year in the county jail *or* a fine not to exceed $4,000 *or* both such confinement and fine.
- Class B misdemeanor: confinement not to exceed 180 days in the county jail *or* a fine not to exceed $2,000 *or* both such confinement and fine.
- Class C misdemeanor: no confinement; a fine not to exceed $500.

CORPORATIONS AND ASSOCIATIONS For a corporation or association convicted of a crime, the court may impose a fine as follows:

- All felonies: a fine up to $20,000.
- Class A or B misdemeanors: a fine up to $10,000.
- Class C misdemeanor: a fine up to $2,000.
- A felony or Class A misdemeanor involving serious bodily injury or death: a fine up to $50,000.

As an alternative, the court can impose a fine up to double any economic gain or loss created by the illegal conduct.

ENHANCEMENTS Punishment ranges may increase when a defendant has prior convictions. Use of prior convictions in this manner is called "enhancement." Enhancements must be set out in the original indictment or information and proved in court.

A Prior Felony Conviction That Resulted in a Prison Sentence If the defendant has a prior felony conviction that resulted in a prison sentence, the following enhancements apply:

- A third-degree felony becomes a second-degree felony.
- A second-degree felony becomes a first-degree felony.
- A first-degree felony has its minimum punishment increased from 5 to 15 years in prison.

Two or More Prior Felony Convictions In the case of two or more prior felony convictions, these must both have resulted in prison sentences and all three crimes must have occurred in sequence. The defendant must have committed Crime No. 1, been sentenced and released from prison, then committed Crime No. 2, been sentenced and released from prison, and then committed Crime No. 3. In this case, the punishment for Crime No. 3 ranges from 25 to 99 years or life.

Two exceptions occur with this enhancement when Crime No. 3 is a state jail felony. First, if Crime No. 3 is a state jail felony, but Nos. 1 and 2 are regular felonies, the punishment increases to a second-degree felony range rather than 25 years to life. Second, if all three crimes are state jail felonies, even if No. 1 and No. 2 were not in sequence, the punishment would increase to only a third-degree felony.

Habitual Sex Offender The section on habitual sex offenders provides for an automatic life sentence for a defendant convicted of aggravated sexual assault, aggravated kidnapping with a sexual motive, or burglary with a sexual motive if the defendant has one prior felony conviction for a sex crime. For purposes of this section only, deferred adjudication and probations, along with prison sentences, count as felony convictions.

A Prior Conviction for Certain Violent Offenses Enhancements apply if the defendant has a prior conviction for certain violent offenses—murder, aggravated kidnapping, aggravated robbery, aggravated sexual assault, indecency with a child by contact, and any felony with a finding that a deadly weapon was used. In such cases, a state jail felony punishment increases to a third-degree felony. A state jail felony also becomes a third-degree felony if the jury finds that the defendant used or exhibited a deadly weapon while committing the crime.

Misdemeanors Misdemeanor punishments can also be enhanced. If a defendant charged with a Class A misdemeanor has a prior conviction for a Class A misdemeanor or any felony, the punishment range becomes 90 days to 1 year with an optional maximum fine of up to $4,000. If a defendant charged with a Class B misdemeanor has a prior conviction for a Class A or B misdemeanor or any felony, the punishment range becomes 30 to 180 days with an optional maximum fine of up to $2,000.

DEFENSES *Defenses* are legal means to avoid punishment even though the defendant committed the crime. They are the legal way of saying, "Yes, I did the crime *but* . . ."

INSANITY Victims sometimes see the insanity plea as a huge legal loophole by which criminals escape the consequences of their crimes. Texas, however, has a very narrow insanity defense that is difficult to establish. In fact, it is rarely successful.

To be legally insane, defendants must suffer a severe mental disease or defect that made them not know that their conduct was wrong. Repeated criminal or antisocial conduct is not evidence of insanity. Defendants have the burden of proving insanity. They must prove it by a preponderance of the evidence. They must also file a written notice of their intent to use this defense at least 10 days before trial.

Establishing that defendants did not know that conduct was wrong is very difficult. In most crimes, they will flee the scene, throw away the weapon, or otherwise cover up the crime. Such conduct indicates that they knew their actions were wrong.

INSANITY: NO LONGER A LOOPHOLE

How tough is it to prove insanity in Texas? Consider the case of Andrea Yates. The nation was shocked in 2001 when it learned the Houston homemaker had drowned her five young children, one by one, in their bathtub. "Surely she must be insane," was heard frequently. Indeed, the jurors at her trial heard evidence and agreed she was psychotic. But that's only half of what must be proved. The jurors also concluded that Yates knew right from wrong. The result? They rejected her insanity defense, found her guilty, and sentenced her to life in prison.

ENTRAPMENT *Entrapment* means that a law enforcement officer induced or persuaded someone to commit a crime. Merely giving someone an opportunity to commit a crime—such as offering to buy or sell drugs—is not entrapment. Defendants use this defense in cases where crucial evidence came from drug- or vice-squad undercover activity.

DURESS *Duress* means that defendants committed crimes only because they were forced to by an imminent threat of serious bodily injury to themselves or another. The threat must be such that it would cause a normal person to give in and commit the crime.

INTOXICATION Voluntary intoxication is not a legal defense in Texas. If intoxication rises to the level of temporary insanity, it may be used as mitigating evidence at the punishment phase. The judge or jury can—but does not have to—use it to decide to lengthen or shorten defendants' sentences.

SELF-DEFENSE Complex laws govern self-defense. It is available to protect oneself against unlawful use of force. Self-defense must be reasonable and immediately necessary. It can include deadly force to prevent someone else from using deadly force or from committing aggravated kidnapping, murder, sexual assault, aggravated sexual assault, robbery, or aggravated robbery.

Self-defense can also be used to protect property. Force, but not deadly force, may be used if it is reasonably necessary to stop a trespass or other interference with property. Deadly force may be used to reasonably prevent arson, burglary, robbery, aggravated robbery, theft during the night, or criminal mischief during the night.

Other specific self-defense provisions define when law enforcement officers can use force.

In general, self-defense is not available if defendants

- are responding to verbal provocation
- are resisting most searches and arrests
- consented to the exact force used
- provoked the force
- armed themselves and sought an explanation or discussion with someone with whom they had a difference

SPECIAL RELATIONSHIPS The law also recognizes that reasonable force may be used in three special relationships when and to the degree necessary to promote discipline or welfare. These relationships are:

- parent-child
- educator-student
- guardian-incompetent

ADDITIONAL LAWS Two additional laws, asset forfeiture and nuisance abatement, are not technically criminal laws but deserve discussion here. They are both highly effective crime-fighting tools.

Asset Forfeiture Law enforcement agencies may seize apparent profits or items they suspect were used in the commission of a crime. They may sell or otherwise use the items for law enforcement purposes. The law was originally designed to fight drugs, but it was expanded in 1991 to include many other types of crimes.

Contraband Law enforcement agencies can declare as contraband any asset used to commit

- any first- or second-degree felony
- any felony robbery, burglary, theft, fraud, or money laundering
- any felony drug offense
- various other felonies such as securities fraud

Proceeds from any of the above offenses or property acquired from the proceeds of any of the above offenses are also contraband.

Procedure After a law enforcement agency seizes such property, the prosecutor representing the state (in most cases, the local district attorney) has 30 days to file a lawsuit. This lawsuit is handled much like any other lawsuit. If the owner contests the lawsuit, the prosecutor for the state must prove by a preponderance of the evidence that the property was contraband. Some procedures are designed to protect innocent owners and lien holders, for example, a car-financing company which provided the loan to purchase a vehicle.

When assets are forfeited, they are divided between the prosecuting agency and the law enforcement agencies that participated in the seizure. The exact division of the property (who gets which item or the percentage division of any cash) is made according to a local agreement between the prosecutor and the law enforcement agencies. Typically, these agreements provide that the prosecutor receive 20% to 50%. The law enforcement agencies split the remainder.

Any money forfeited gets deposited in the state, county, or municipal treasury subject to the normal accounting procedures of each governmental unit. Law enforcement agencies must spend their money for law enforcement purposes; prosecutors may spend their money on any official purpose of their office. The governing body of the law enforcement agency or the prosecutor's office may spend up to 10% of any money for certain drug prevention or treatment programs.

Nuisance Abatement Another set of highly effective law enforcement tools are the nuisance abatement statutes. Although they have been on the books for years, problems associated with drugs—particularly crack cocaine—have led to the recent aggressive use of these laws. Nuisance abatement laws allow law enforcement agencies to obtain court orders requiring property owners to take steps to end repeated criminal conduct on their property. If the owners are not successful in doing so, the court can order the property padlocked for up to one year.

Four separate nuisance laws, separately or in combination, are triggered by repeated

- illegal gambling
- prostitution
- pornography sale or exhibition
- live sex shows
- reckless discharge of firearms
- criminal street gang activity
- illegal drug activity
- violations of the Alcoholic Beverage Code

A local district attorney, county attorney, or city attorney may file a lawsuit against the owner of the property (who may not be the owner of the business). Property owners are responsible for their property. If a court finds that any of the above violations occur at the property, the court may order the property closed for one year. The owners may continue to operate if they post a bond as set by the court up to $10,000. For an additional violation, the court may forfeit the bond and begin the one-year closure. Also, those who violate the court's order are subject to a fine of up to $10,000 and a jail term of up to 30 days.

"TURN AROUND TEXAS": CITIZEN INVOLVEMENT THAT WORKS

Mae Willie Turner and Gladys Hubbard, two active sisters in their late 70's, lived together in a house in Taylor, Texas. Taylor is a small central Texas town of about 10,000 citizens, the

kind of small town where people are supposed to be able to enjoy peace and quiet.

But in the fall of 1993, Turner and Hubbard's neighborhood was held hostage to drugs and gangs. Drugs were dealt openly on the street, four murders occurred in a two-block area, gunfire was common, gambling rampant, and gang members stopped traffic at will.

In October 1994 dozens of Taylor drug dealers were rounded up and charged with delivery of cocaine. Very few of them were able to make the high bonds that were set in the Williamson County Courts and ultimately all of the dealers were convicted and received prison sentences that averaged 27 years.

It was the type of drug arrest that had been made many times before—the type that makes big headlines but brings a neighborhood only a few weeks of peace before a new crop of dealers is in place.

This time, though, the neighborhood was fed up. A small community group had been meeting with Police Chief Fred Stansbury at a local church. In November they invited several people, myself included, to offer ideas on what could be done. The bottom line of each suggestion was that the community needed to get, and stay, involved.

A first task was to file lawsuits against four Taylor bars that were breeding grounds for much of the criminal activity—violence, gambling, and drug dealing. Within a few months and with citizen demonstrations of support, all four bars were permanently closed. As marches continued, the Texas National Guard joined in the effort and began demolishing abandoned houses and businesses that fostered drug dealing and use.

The Taylor program then caught the attention of state officials. In the spring of 1995, Governor George W. Bush led 1,000 school children down the main street, a parade that concluded with National Guard demolition of a crack house.

Marches, vigils, bar closures, crack house demolition, a new police substation, a police athletic league, and a renewed community all came out of Turn Around Taylor. The program, renamed Turn Around Texas and now having state funding and the governor's active support, has been utilized in Athens, Corsicana, Elgin, Greenville, Kilgore, Longview, La Marque/Texas City, Plainview, and Waxahachie.

As for Taylor, the program continued until its job was

complete. Violent crime in Mae Turner and Gladys Hubbard's neighborhood was down 80%, vandalism 90%, a new church and several retail establishments were built where drugs were formerly sold, and two very determined senior citizens, who were some of the most faithful marchers, could sit on their front porch each night and enjoy the peace and quiet.

SPECIFIC CRIMES The Texas Penal Code and the Controlled Substances Act define more than a hundred crimes. Many of these crimes have substantial subsections that carry different punishments. These subsections included, Texas criminal law defines several hundred crimes. This chapter lists the ones actually prosecuted in the order they appear in the Penal Code and then the Controlled Substances Act. A few obscure crimes, such as illegal recruitment of an athlete, are seldom if ever prosecuted and are not included here.

MURDER RATE DECLINES

Texans have been shocked by many brutal murders over the past few years. Indeed, some nightly newscasts seem as if they could more accurately be termed the nightly murder cast.

Murder statistics, however, show a different picture. Murder is nearly always reported to law enforcement. Yet, murder rates peaked in the years from 1979–1982, went back to nearly the same levels in 1990–91, then fell dramatically in the rest of the 1990s and have held steady for the past seven years at an historically low rate. The 2003 murder rate in Texas, along with the murder rates from 1997–2002, are the lowest recorded since the early 1960s.

Let me quickly add that 1,417 murders at a rate of 6.4 per 100,000 citizens in 2003 is an unacceptably high level of murders. It is, however, vastly better than the 2,651 murders in 1991 or the murder rate of 16.9 per 100,000 citizens in 1980. The number of murders and murder rate for Texas since 1979 is shown below:

Year	*Murders*	*Rate/100,000 pop.*
1979	2,226	16.6
1980	2,389	16.9
1981	2,438	16.5
1982	2,463	16.1
1983	2,238	14.2
1984	2,091	13.1

Year	*Murders*	*Rate/100,000 pop.*
1985	2,124	13.0
1986	2,256	13.5
1987	1,960	11.7
1988	2,021	12.0
1989	2,029	11.9
1990	2,388	14.1
1991	2,651	15.3
1992	2,239	12.7
1993	2,149	11.9
1994	2,023	11.0
1995	1,694	9.0
1996	1,476	7.7
1997	1,328	6.8
1998	1,343	6.8
1999	1,218	6.1
2000	1,236	6.9
2001	1,331	6.2
2002	1,305	6.0
2003	1,417	6.4

HOMICIDE *Homicide* is the unlawful taking of another individual's life. The law defines an individual as a person who was born and is alive. Assaults on pregnant women that result in a death of a fetus can be prosecuted only as a crime against the woman. (For intoxication manslaughter, see the section below on intoxication offenses.)

Murder A murderer either

- intends to cause or knowingly causes the death, or
- does not intend the death but does intend serious bodily injury and commits an act clearly dangerous to human life, or
- does not intend the death but does intend some other felony and commits an act clearly dangerous to human life

Murder is a first-degree felony. However, at the punishment phase, murderers may offer proof that they killed under the immediate influence of sudden passion arising from an adequate cause. If the jury finds this to be true, the crime becomes a second-degree felony.

REAL KILLERS/REAL CRIMES

It is difficult to discuss the death penalty without considering the actual heinousness of capital crimes. What do we execute for? Consider the first five defendants executed in 2003:

Samuel Clark Gallamore (Kerr County). Gallamore was a crack addict who broke into a home in rural Kerr County. Once inside, he and a co-defendant beat and stabbed to death 83-year-old Clayton Kenney, his partially paralyzed 74-year-old wife, Julianna, and their 44-year-old daughter. Gallamore then stole cash, silver, and other valuables. His motive was to obtain more money to buy crack. Gallamore murdered the elderly couple and their daughter on March 29, 1992; he was executed on January 14, 2003—10 years, 9 months, and 16 days later.

John Richard Baltazar (Nueces County). Baltazar, who had been paroled from prison two months earlier, broke into a Corpus Christi home looking for a man who had moved out a week earlier. He opened fire and killed 5-year-old Adriana Marines as she was curled up on her family's couch watching *Sleeping Beauty*. He also wounded a 10-year-old girl and an adult man. Baltazar killed the 5-year-old girl on September 27, 1997; he was executed on January 15, 2003—5 years, 3 months, and 19 days later.

Robert Andrew Lookingbill (Hidalgo County). Lookingbill beat his 70-year-old grandmother to death while she slept. He also bludgeoned his grandfather with the same steel pipe. His grandfather survived in a coma for about a year before dying. Lookingbill's grandparents had taken him in about a year and a half earlier, when he was released from prison on parole. Lookingbill killed his grandmother on December 5, 1989; he was executed on January 22, 2003—13 years, 1 month, and 17 days later.

Alva Curry (Travis County). Curry was a gang member and two-bit drug dealer when he robbed an Austin convenience store. Even though the 20-year-old clerk, David Vela, cooperated and gave Curry and an accomplice $220, Curry shot him five times. Vela died from the gunshots. Seven days later, Curry killed another clerk in a convenience store robbery that netted $71.15. Curry shot David Vela to death on October 16, 1991; he was executed on January 28, 2003—11 years, 3 months, and 12 days later.

Richard Eugene Dinkins (Jefferson County). Dinkins, upset because he had written a hot check for a massage treatment, went back to the clinic, where he shot the 44-year-old owner

and nurse, Katherine Thompson. He then broke down a door into an office where another nurse, 32-year-old Shelly Cutler, had fled. He shot her in the head also. Both women died. Dinkins murdered the women on September 12, 1990; he was executed on January 29, 2003—12 years, 4 months, and 17 days later.

Capital Murder Capital murder is an intentional murder under one of eight special circumstances:

- murder of an on-duty peace officer or firefighter
- murder while committing kidnapping, burglary, robbery, aggravated sexual assault, arson, obstruction or retaliation, or certain types of terroristic threats
- murder for hire
- murder while escaping from a prison or jail
- murder by a prison or jail inmate either of an employee or as part of gang activity
- murder while incarcerated for murder or capital murder or while serving life or 99 years for aggravated kidnapping, aggravated sexual assault, or aggravated robbery
- murder of more than one person during the same transaction or scheme
- murder of a child under six

Capital murder is punishable by either life imprisonment or death. At the punishment phase of a capital murder trial, the jury answers two questions:

- Is the murderer a continuing threat to society?
- Does mitigating evidence justify a sentence of life imprisonment rather than the death penalty?

Mitigating evidence includes the circumstances of the offense and the murderer's character and background. If the jury answers "yes" to the first question and "no" to the second, the judge sentences the murderer to death. If the jury answers either "no" to the first question or "yes" to the second, the judge sentences the murderer to life in prison.

Also, the U.S. Supreme Court has ruled that a person with mental retardation cannot be given the death penalty. If there is evidence of retardation, the jury answers a third question:

- Is the murderer a person with mental retardation?

In Texas "mental retardation" means significant subaverage intellect coupled with very low independent living and social skills. If the jury answers this third question "yes," the judge must sentence the murderer to life in prison.

Manslaughter A person recklessly—rather than intentionally or knowingly—causes the death of an individual. *Recklessly* means a major departure from acceptable conduct, such as driving a car 100 miles per hour in a school zone. Manslaughter is a second-degree felony.

Criminally Negligent Homicide A person negligently causes the death of an individual. A negligent defendant was not but should have been aware of a major departure from acceptable conduct. For example, the defendant failed to place an infant in a car seat before a collision that resulted in the infant's death. Criminally negligent homicide is a state jail felony.

TEXAS LEADS THE NATION

From 1976 until May 2004 there were 909 executions in the United States. Roughly a third of these were in Texas. The number of executions by state:

Texas	321
Virginia	91
Oklahoma	73
Missouri	61
Florida	58
Georgia	34
North Carolina	31
South Carolina	31
Alabama	28
Louisiana	27
Arkansas	26
Arizona	22
Delaware	13
Illinois	12
Indiana	11
Ohio	11
Nevada	10
California	10

Fourteen states had executed less than ten murderers: Mississippi (6); Utah (6); Washington (4); Nebraska (3); Pennsylvania (3); Maryland (3); Kentucky (2); Montana (2); Oregon (2); Colorado (1); Idaho (1); New Mexico (1); Tennessee (1); and Wyoming (1).

Source: NAACP Legal Defense and Education Fund

KIDNAPPING AND UNLAWFUL RESTRAINT

Kidnapping A kidnapper takes or holds a person against his or her will and either uses deadly force or hides the victim. It is not kidnapping for relatives to peaceably assume lawful control of a child. Kidnapping is a third-degree felony.

Aggravated Kidnapping Kidnapping becomes aggravated kidnapping when it is used

- for ransom or reward
- for a shield or hostage
- as part of a felony
- to physically injure or sexually abuse the victim
- to terrorize the victim or another
- to interfere with a governmental or political function

Kidnapping also becomes aggravated when the kidnapper uses or exhibits a deadly weapon. Aggravated kidnapping is a first-degree felony. At the punishment phase of the trial, kidnappers may offer evidence that they voluntarily released the victim in a safe place. If the jury finds this to be true, the crime becomes a second-degree felony.

Unlawful Restraint In a slightly less serious crime, a kidnapper holds another person against his or her will. Unlike kidnapping, unlawful restraint does not involve deadly force or hiding the victim. However, relatives may peaceably assume lawful control of a child. Unlawful restraint is a Class B misdemeanor. If the victim is under 14, unlawful restraint is a Class A misdemeanor. If the victim is exposed to a substantial risk of serious bodily injury, it becomes a third-degree felony.

CHILD MOLESTING *Child molesting*, a general term, refers to any sexual offense against a child. The age of the victim at the time of the offense helps define the crime. For this purpose, a person is legally a child until his or her seventeenth birthday.

CHILD SEXUAL ABUSE

To the casual observer, it seems that child sexual abuse suddenly began in the early 1980s. Before then, child molesters were seldom reported and, when reported, seldom investigated or prosecuted aggressively. Now we investigate, we prosecute, and we confine the molesters.

What happened? In 1984 a TV movie, *Something About Amelia,* stirred the national consciousness—and conscience. Almost overnight, we passed laws, developed investigation techniques, trained social workers and law enforcement officers, and learned how to try such cases.

Are adults molesting children less frequently as a result of increased public awareness and more aggressive law enforcement? The number of reported cases and ongoing prosecutions of child sexual abuse show that the problem has not diminished. (My former office in Williamson County handled several dozen cases each year.)

What can we do? Our response must be first to convict and incarcerate as many child molesters as possible. Second, we must recognize that while such abuse has always existed, it is currently aggravated by some combination of increased divorce rates, increased mobility, drug abuse, and, most certainly, the increase in live-in boyfriends. Only when we acknowledge and deal with these factors can we hope to see a significant downturn in child sexual abuse.

Indecency with a Child Indecency with a child can either be by contact or by exposure.

- *by contact* means touching for sexual purposes the anus, breast, or any part of the genitals of a child younger than 17.
- *by exposure* means exposure for sexual purposes of the anus or any part of the genitals knowing that a child under 17 is present.

In either case, the child's consent is not relevant. It is no defense that the child acquiesced or even initiated the incident.

There are two exceptions to the "under 17" rule. Spouses cannot be victims. Also, a defendant can use as a defense the fact that he or she was not more than three years older than the victim and did not use force or threats.

Indecency by contact is a second-degree felony. Indecency by exposure is a third-degree felony.

Sexual Assault of a Child During sexual assault, a sexual organ or an object penetrates or contacts a mouth, anus, or other sexual organ. The victim must be a child under age 17 and not be the spouse of the defendant.

As with indecency with a child, consent is not an issue. Again, the defendant can use as a defense the fact that he or she was not more than three years older than the victim and did not use force or threats.

In the past, defendants could use a promiscuity defense if the victim was 14 years or older, but this was eliminated after August 31, 1994.

Sexual assault of a child is a second-degree felony.

Aggravated Sexual Assault of a Child Sexual assault of a child becomes aggravated sexual assault when the victim is younger than 14. As with other child-molesting laws, consent is not an issue. Aggravated sexual assault is a first-degree felony.

ASHLEY'S LAWS

It was Labor Day, September 6, 1993. The Estell family—mom, dad, big brother, and 7-year-old Ashley—were with hundreds of others in Plano that day enjoying youth soccer games. While watching her brother play his game, Ashley simply disappeared.

Her body was discovered a few days later. A police investigation led to the arrest of a paroled sex offender, Michael Blair. Because of the resulting publicity and strong feelings against Blair, the trial was moved to Midland.

District Attorney Tom O'Connell led the prosecution team and obtained a conviction and death sentence against Blair. O'Connell would later comment that this was "one of the most emotionally draining prosecutions of my career—one that literally devastated the community."

But conviction and sentence would not bring Ashley back. State Senator Florence Shapiro and others began to ask questions about how a convicted sex offender could be out after serving only 18 months. Despite disciplinary problems in prison, Blair had still received an early release on a burglary conviction. Parole officials claimed they were unaware that Blair had a sex offense conviction.

In response, Shapiro crafted a package of legislative reforms that ultimately became known as Ashley's Laws. Ashley's parents, District Attorney O'Connell, and a number of other Plano and Collin County officials came to Austin and

testified in favor of the legislation. In all, 12 bills passed through the legislature and, on May 29, 1995, Governor George W. Bush signed the bills into law.

Ashley's Laws include:

- ***limits on prison good time*—prohibits prison officials from returning good-time credits taken away from an inmate because of disciplinary actions.**
- ***mandatory life sentences for habitual sex offenders*—requires an automatic life sentence for anyone convicted of a first-degree sex offense who has two prior convictions, at least one of which is a sex offense. (This was later toughened further by requiring only one prior felony conviction for a sex offense rather than two felony convictions.) The offender sentenced to life would not be eligible for parole for 35 calendar years. Any parole decision would require a two-thirds vote of the entire 18-member parole board.**
- ***public notification and sex offender registration*—requires both registration of sex offenders before they are released and notification in a local newspaper that a sex offender is about to be released.**
- ***victim notification*—requires officials to notify the victim when an inmate escapes from prison or is placed on probation.**
- ***victim appearance before parole board*—gives the victim the right to appear personally before the parole board votes on an offender's release.**
- ***community supervision requirements*—mandates that the trial judge impose conditions on any probation of a sex offender. The offender cannot participate in programs that include children and cannot go near places where children gather, such as schools, parks, and swimming pools.**

SEXUAL OFFENSES

Sexual Assault Sexual assaults, or rapes, fall under either the sexual assault or aggravated sexual assault laws. Unlike child-molesting laws, which protect children under 17, sexual assault laws stipulate that consent is an issue. The state must prove a lack of consent. A rapist knowingly or intentionally

- penetrates the anus or female sexual organ by any means
- penetrates the victim's mouth with the assailant's sexual organ

- causes the victim's sexual organ to contact or penetrate the mouth, anus, or sexual organ of the assailant or any other person

What is lack of consent? Legally, it's when the assailant

- uses physical force or violence
- threatens force or violence that the victim believes could be carried out
- knows the victim is unconscious or physically unable to resist
- knows the victim is mentally infirm and unable to resist or understand what is happening
- knows the victim is unaware the sexual assault is happening
- has given the victim a substance, without the victim's knowledge, that impairs the victim's ability to understand or resist
- threatens force or violence to another person that the victim believes could be carried out
- is a public servant who coerces the victim to submit or participate
- is a mental health provider or member of the clergy who has sex with a person by exploiting the victim's emotional dependency on the provider or clergyperson

Evidence of previous sexual conduct of the victim is generally not admissible in a trial involving a sexual assault. A narrow exception allows such evidence

- when the defense is rebutting (explaining) scientific or medical evidence offered by the prosecutor
- when the previous sexual conduct was with the defendant and is relevant to consent
- when the evidence relates to a motive or bias of the victim

Defense lawyers who want to ask such questions must first have the judge hear the evidence without the jury present. The judge must find that the evidence meets one of these exceptions before the jury can hear these questions answered. Sexual assault is a second-degree felony.

Aggravated Sexual Assault Sexual assault becomes aggravated sexual assault when the assailant

- causes serious bodily injury or attempts to kill the victim or someone else

- by acts or words places the victim in fear that death, serious bodily injury, or kidnapping will immediately happen to the victim or someone else
- by acts or words in the presence of the victim threatens the death, serious bodily injury, or kidnapping of any person
- uses or exhibits a deadly weapon

Assault also becomes aggravated when the victim is age 65 or older. Aggravated sexual assault is a first-degree felony.

50% more rapes are committed in August than in December. The occurrence of rape increases dramatically for all of the summer months.

Source: Texas Department of Public Safety

Public Lewdness Public lewdness occurs when two or more people engage in sexual conduct in either a public place or a private place where the people are reckless about whether the conduct will offend or alarm someone else who is present. The offense also includes sexual conduct between one or more people and an animal or fowl. Public lewdness is a Class A misdemeanor.

Indecent Exposure In indecent exposure, a person recklessly exposes his or her genitals or anus with the intent to sexually arouse any other person. The defendant must have been reckless about whether his or her action would alarm or offend another person who is present. Indecent exposure is a Class B misdemeanor.

ASSAULT In assault, an assailant knowingly or intentionally

- causes bodily injury to the victim, a Class A misdemeanor
- threatens imminent bodily injury, a Class C misdemeanor
- causes an offensive or provocative contact to the victim, a Class C misdemeanor

Bodily injury means physical pain, illness, or any impairment of physical condition.

Aggravated Assault An assault becomes aggravated when the bodily injury is serious or the assailant uses or exhibits a deadly weapon while committing the assault. What is serious bodily injury? It includes death or any injury that creates a substantial risk of death, serious permanent disfigurement, or protracted loss or impairment of the function of any bodily member or organ.

Most aggravated assaults are second-degree felonies. They become first-degree felonies if

- the assailant is a public servant acting within his or her employment
- the victim is known by the assailant to be a public servant (or security guard) performing his or her duties
- the assailant is retaliating for some official duty carried out by the public servant
- the assailant is retaliating against a victim because the victim reported a crime or served as a witness, prospective witness, or informant

A *public servant* is any employee or agent of government, including jurors, grand jurors, and candidates for election to public office.

Injury to a Child, Elderly Individual, or Disabled Individual Injury to a child, elderly individual, or disabled individual involves bodily or mental injury. A person may act intentionally, knowingly, recklessly, or with criminal negligence. This crime, like most, requires an action, but it can also be committed by failing to do something that a person has a legal obligation to do. For example, it is a crime for a parent to starve a young child.

Each of the three classes of victims has a specific definition. Children are under 15. Elderly individuals are 65 or older. Disabled individuals are over 14 and unable to protect or care for themselves.

OTHER CONDUCT THAT CAUSES INJURY

Abandoning or Endangering a Child The crime of abandoning or endangering a child involves a person with care or control of the child intentionally leaving the child in a place that exposes the child to an unreasonable risk of harm. To endanger a child, a person either does something or fails to do something that places a child in imminent danger of physical or mental injury. Abandonment is a third-degree felony unless the person who committed the crime intended to return to the child, in which case it becomes a state jail felony. Abandonment is a second-degree felony if a reasonable person would believe the child was in imminent danger of physical or mental injury. Endangering a child is a state jail felony.

Deadly Conduct The offense of deadly conduct originally prohibited reckless conduct that placed another in imminent danger of serious bodily injury. In 1993, the legislature expanded the offense to include discharging a firearm toward people or a vehicle, building, or habitation. The defendant had to be reckless about whether the vehicle, building, or habitation was occupied. The expanded law covers drive-by shootings where the facts do not show the specific intent to murder. The original deadly conduct offense is a Class A misdemeanor. The discharge-of-firearm addition makes it a third-degree felony.

Terroristic Threat A threat to commit any violent crime (such as a bomb scare) is in itself a crime of terroristic threat. If the terrorist intended to strike fear of imminent serious bodily injury or to cause an emergency agency (such as police or fire departments) to respond, the crime is a Class B misdemeanor. If the terrorist intended to interrupt the use of a place (such as emptying a building by issuing a bomb threat), the crime is classified as a Class A misdemeanor. If the terrorist intended to interrupt a public utility (such as water, gas, or communications), the crime is a third-degree felony.

Aiding Suicide In the crime of aiding a suicide, a person helps someone who either tries to commit or does commit suicide. Aiding suicide is a Class C misdemeanor. However, if the defendant's actions actually caused either the successful suicide or an attempted suicide that results in serious bodily injury, the crime is a state jail felony.

Tampering with a Consumer Product Tampering with a consumer product involves a person adding to or altering a consumer product to make it likely that someone will suffer death or serious bodily injury. Tampering is a second-degree felony unless someone dies or suffers serious bodily injury, in which case it becomes a first-degree felony. A threat to tamper with intent to cause fear or injury or to hurt product sales is a third-degree felony.

Leaving a Child in a Vehicle A child under the age of 7 must not be left in a motor vehicle for more than five minutes without someone at least 14 years or older remaining in the vehicle to look after the child. Leaving a child in a vehicle is a Class C misdemeanor.

FAMILY OFFENSES

Bigamy A bigamist is married to more than one person at a time. A reasonable belief that any prior marriage was dissolved by death, divorce, or annulment is a defense. Bigamy is a Class A misdemeanor.

Incest Incest involves certain family members engaging in sexual acts with each other. These family members include parents, grandparents, and children by both blood or adoption, stepparents and stepchildren while the marriage exists, and aunts, uncles, brothers, sisters, nieces, and nephews. Incest prosecutions normally involve adults; if one of the participants is a child, child-molesting statutes normally provide a more severe punishment. Incest is a third-degree felony.

Interference with Child Custody Interference with child custody occurs when a person

- takes or keeps a child in violation of a court custody order
- takes a child out of the geographical area of a court while knowing that a custody lawsuit (such as a divorce) has been filed
- is the parent without custody and entices or persuades a child to leave the person with custody

Interference with child custody is a state jail felony.

Enticing a Child The crime of enticing a child occurs when a person entices, persuades, or takes a child from a court-ordered custodian. Enticing a child is a Class B misdemeanor.

Criminal Nonsupport A person commits criminal nonsupport if he or she fails to support his or her children. Inability to pay is a defense. Criminal nonsupport is a state jail felony.

Harboring a Runaway A person harbors a runaway if that runaway is a child under 18 years of age and the person is negligent about whether or not the child has run away from home or escaped from a peace officer, probation officer, or similar situation. Harboring a runaway is a Class A misdemeanor.

Violation of a Protective Order A protective order is a court order to stop domestic violence by commanding that a person not go near or communicate with another member of the family. Violation of such an order occurs when a person commits family violence, communicates with the other person, or goes to the prohibited places, such as residence, workplace, or school. Violating a protective order is a Class A misdemeanor. A third conviction under this section is a state jail felony.

Sale or Purchase of a Child The sale or purchase of a child occurs when a person sells or purchases a child for purposes of adoption. Exceptions are made for fees paid to a lawful child-placing agency and for payment or reimbursement of proper legal and medical bills. Selling or purchasing a child is a third-degree felony.

DESTRUCTION OF PROPERTY

Arson An arsonist starts a fire or causes an explosion with the intent to either damage or destroy a habitation, building, vehicle, vegetation, fence, or structure. If the property is a habitation, building, or vehicle, it must be located within an incorporated city or town. Also, the arson must affect someone else's economic interest (belong to someone else, be insured or mortgaged, etc.), or the arsonist must have been reckless about whether the burning or explosion would endanger the life of some individual or the safety of another's property. Arson is a second-degree felony. If anyone is hurt or killed, the crime becomes a first-degree felony.

7,645 arsons were reported in 2003. Property damage from these arsons amounted to more than $105 million.

Source: Texas Department of Public Safety, Crime in Texas, 2003

Criminal Mischief A person who, without the consent of the owner, engages in the following activities commits criminal mischief:

- intentionally damages or destroys another's property
- intentionally tampers with another's property, causing economic loss or substantial inconvenience
- marks on another's property (including drawing or painting, etc.)

Criminal mischief ranges from a Class C misdemeanor (for under $20 worth of damage) to a first-degree felony (for $200,000 or more worth of damage). The values and the punishments are the same as those under the theft statute.

ROBBERY OFFENSES A robber takes property from a victim by force or threat. Robbery is often confused with burglary and theft. A burglar enters a vehicle or structure to commit a crime, and a thief takes property or services.

Robbery A robber, in the course of committing theft,

- causes bodily injury to another
- threatens or places another in fear of imminent bodily injury or death

Robbery is a second-degree felony.

Aggravated Robbery Robbery becomes aggravated when the robber

- causes serious bodily injury to a victim
- uses or exhibits a deadly weapon
- robs an older (over 65) or disabled person

Aggravated robbery is a first-degree felony.

BURGLARY

Burglary of a Building Burglary of a building occurs when a person enters a building and either intends to or does commit any felony or theft. This definition can include a portion of a building not open to the public. The entry must be without the consent of the owner.

The classification of the burglary depends on the type of structure entered and the intent of the burglar:

- Burglary is a state jail felony if the burglar enters a building other than a habitation.
- Burglary of a habitation (any structure or vehicle adapted for overnight use by people) is a second-degree felony if the burglar intended to commit theft.
- Burglary of a habitation is a first-degree felony if the burglar intended to commit any felony other than theft. For example, some house burglars intend to commit sexual assault or other acts of violence.

Burglary of a Vehicle The burglar of a vehicle enters a vehicle or part of a vehicle with intent to commit a felony or theft. The entry must be without consent of the owner. Burglary of a vehicle is a Class A misdemeanor unless it involves a rail car, in which case it is a state jail felony.

Criminal Trespass In criminal trespass, a trespasser enters or remains on property or in a building without consent of the owner or person in charge of the property. The trespasser must have notice to leave or notice that entry is forbidden. This notice can be given by:

- oral or written communication to the trespasser
- fencing or other enclosure obviously designed to exclude intruders
- a sign indicating that trespass is forbidden

Criminal trespass is a Class B misdemeanor. It becomes a Class A misdemeanor if it happens in a habitation or if the defendant has a deadly weapon.

CRIME RATES

Newspaper headlines frequently talk about increases or decreases in the crime rate. Most likely they are referring to statistics collected as part of the Uniform Crime Reporting (UCR) program.

The UCR program was begun by the FBI in the 1930s as a way to standardize crime reporting and obtain national crime data. Nearly all police agencies in the country now report crime information to the UCR program.

The major component of the UCR program is the standardized reporting of the seven major index crimes.

***Murder*—willful killing of one human being by another**

***Rape*—carnal knowledge of a female forcibly and against her will**

***Robbery*—taking or attempting to take anything of value from a person by force, by the threat of force or violence, or by putting the victim in fear**

***Aggravated Assault*—unlawful attack by one person upon another for the purpose of inflicting severe or aggravated bodily injury**

***Burglary*—unlawful entry of a structure with intent to commit a felony or a theft**

***Theft*—unlawful taking, carrying, leading, or riding away of property from the possession or constructive possession of another**

***Motor Vehicle Theft*—theft or attempted theft of a motor vehicle, excluding motor boats, construction equipment, airplanes, and farming equipment**

THEFT Texas' theft laws cover a wide range of taking another's property, including various forms of fraud. Theft can involve property (such as real estate or personal property) or services (such as labor or hotel lodging).

Theft of Property Theft requires some form of taking or transferring control of property. Theft also requires at least one of the following additional circumstances, that the thief

- lacks the owner's consent
- receives property he or she knows another stole
- receives property from a law enforcement agent who represented it as stolen

The punishment range for theft depends on the value of the property stolen. A standard value ladder is used for many crimes.

Value Ladder	
Less than $20 (in some cases $50)	Class C misdemeanor
$20 (or $50) to less than $500	Class B misdemeanor
$500 to less than $1,500	Class A misdemeanor
$1,500 to less than $20,000	State jail felony
$20,000 to less than $100,000	Third-degree felony
$100,000 to less than $200,000	Second-degree felony
$200,000 or more	First-degree felony

Value of property is the fair market value of the property when it is stolen. Replacement value can be used only if a fair market value cannot be determined. If the theft is part of an overall scheme or course of conduct, theft amounts can be aggregated or totaled. For example, a defendant who sold 10,000 fake raffle tickets for $1 each could be prosecuted for a single state jail felony rather than 10,000 Class C misdemeanors.

$1.7 billion worth of property was stolen in Texas in 2003. More than one-third of this property was recovered.

Source: Texas Department of Public Safety, Crime in Texas, 2003

Theft of Services The law for theft of services is very similar to the regular theft law. Some special provisions make it easier for prosecutors to prove theft from a hotel, restaurant, or rental property. The value ladder and punishment ranges are the same as under theft.

Unauthorized Use of a Vehicle It is a crime to operate a boat, airplane, or motor-propelled vehicle without the owner's consent. This law is usually used to prosecute vehicle theft because it is necessary to prove only that the thief was operating the vehicle, not that he or she actually took it. The value ladder does not apply to this crime. All unauthorized uses of vehicles are state jail felonies.

No. 1 most likely item to be stolen is a motor vehicle, followed by: (2) electronic equipment (TVs, stereos); (3) jewelry; (4) cash; (5) office equipment.

Source: Texas Department of Public Safety

Forgery A forger creates or alters any writing for the purposes of harming or defrauding another. Passing or possessing with intent to pass a forgery also counts as forgery. Writing includes both printing and any other method of recording information. Forgery is a Class A misdemeanor, with two exceptions. Forgery of a will, deed, check, contract, or similar business document is a state jail felony. Forgery of certain other important documents—such as money, securities, a government-issued license, stocks, or bonds—is a third-degree felony.

8,622 arrests occurred in 2003 for forgery and related offenses.

Source: Texas Department of Public Safety, Crime in Texas, 2003

Credit or Debit Card Abuse Credit or debit card abuse involves a person using someone else's card without permission, using an expired card, or stealing a card. Using a card number instead of the actual card under any of these circumstances is also a crime. Credit or debit card abuse is a state jail felony.

Securing Execution of a Document by Deception The antifraud statute on securing execution of a document by deception is extremely broad. A person harms or defrauds another person by causing that person, through deception, to sign or issue a document that affects that person's economic interest. Thus, any deception that causes another person to write a check or issue a receipt that harms or defrauds that person can be prosecuted under this statute. The classification for this crime ranges from Class C misdemeanor (for affected property worth less than $20) to first-degree felony (for affected property worth $200,000 or more). The values and the punishments are the same as those under the theft statute.

Computer Crimes The statute on computer crimes covers several computer-related activities. A person committing a computer crime

- accesses a computer or computer system without the owner's consent

• gives out a password or other similar information, without the owner's consent, that would allow someone to access restricted information

This crime is a Class A misdemeanor unless the person intends to harm or defraud another. In the case of harm or fraud, the crime is a state jail felony if the economic benefit or harm is less than $20,000; if the benefit or harm is $20,000 or more, the crime is a third-degree felony. Computer crimes can be prosecuted in addition to other offenses such as theft.

Insurance Fraud In insurance fraud a person, with intent to deceive the insurer, presents or prepares an insurance claim that has a significant false statement. The punishment is based on the value ladder contained in the section on theft of property.

PUBLIC CORRUPTION

Bribery A briber exchanges a benefit for another person's decision, such as a vote. The object of the bribe can be any government employee, a political party official, or a voter. Both the offeror and acceptor of the bribe are guilty. Also, it is a crime to solicit a bribe. Political contributions are exempt from the bribery law unless there is direct evidence of a specific agreement to exchange the contribution for a specific vote or action. Bribery is a second-degree felony.

Coercion of Public Servant or Voter In coercion of a public servant or voter, a person makes an illegal threat, such as physical force or economic ruin, to influence some official action of a government employee or voter. Coercion is a Class A misdemeanor unless the person threatens to commit a felony. Then it is a third-degree felony.

Gift to a Public Servant The crime of gift to a public servant involves a government employee accepting a gift from someone with whom that employee deals directly in the course of his or her work. Specific definitions in the statute cover inspectors, jailers, government lawyers, officials who approve contracts or payments, judges, and hearing examiners. For example, a jailer may not solicit or accept a benefit from a prisoner. Members of the legislature and their employees may not accept gifts from any person.

This law is similar to the bribery statute. The chief difference is that the prosecutor does not have to show that the gift was given to obtain a specific action. This section does not apply to political contributions and other items that must be reported by law. Giving a gift to a public servant is a Class A misdemeanor.

Perjury A perjurer makes a false statement under oath. The perjurer must know what the statement means and must intend to deceive. Perjury is a Class A misdemeanor.

Aggravated Perjury Perjury becomes aggravated if committed in connection with an official proceeding, such as a trial, and if it is important to the outcome of the proceeding.

Tampering with a Government Record Tampering with a government record involves a person making a false entry or destroying a government record. Tampering is a Class A misdemeanor unless the person intends to harm or defraud another. Then it becomes a state jail felony. Tampering becomes a third-degree felony if the document is a government-issued license and a second-degree felony if the person tampers with the license with the intent to harm or defraud another.

Abuse of Official Capacity The statute on abuse of official capacity applies to government employees. In this crime, a governmental employee

- violates a law relating to his or her office or employment
- misuses government property, services, or personnel

Abuse of official capacity is a Class A misdemeanor. Punishment ranges from a Class C misdemeanor (value under $20) to a first-degree felony (value $200,000 or more). The values and punishments are the same as those for the theft statute.

A government employee who steals property rather than misuses it can be prosecuted for theft. Theft of government property by a government employee carries a punishment one degree higher in range than any other theft. Thus, a government employee's theft will normally be prosecuted as theft with these special punishment provisions rather than abuse of official capacity.

Violations of Civil Rights of a Person in Custody It is against the law for a peace officer or employee of a correctional facility (such as a jail) to interfere with or deny a civil right or privilege of a person in custody. Violation of these rights is a Class A misdemeanor.

Misuse of Official Information The statute on misuse of official information applies to a government employee who

- uses nonpublic inside information to obtain an economic interest in property or to speculate on the basis of the information
- discloses such nonpublic inside information to obtain a benefit or to harm or defraud another

This statute also applies to a person who solicits or receives this type of information from a government employee in order to obtain a benefit or to harm or defraud another. Misuse of official information is a third-degree felony.

ESCAPE AND CORRECTIONAL FACILITY OFFENSES

Escape It is unlawful for a person to escape from custody. If the escapee is in custody for a felony or escapes from a jail, prison, or similar secure facility, this crime is a third-degree felony. If the escapee uses a deadly weapon or causes serious bodily injury, escape is a first-degree felony. All other escapes are Class A misdemeanors.

Related statutes prohibit permitting, facilitating, or providing implements for an escape. Permitting or facilitating an escape is a Class A misdemeanor unless the escapee is charged with a felony, in which event it is a third-degree felony. If the escapee is confined in a prison or uses a deadly weapon, the crime is a second-degree felony. Providing implements for an escape is a third-degree felony unless the implement is a deadly weapon, in which case this crime is a second-degree felony.

ESCAPE FROM PRISON

They were seven dangerous convicts. Killers, robbers, and rapists. All serving long sentences. All confined at the maximum security Connally Unit near Kenedy in South Texas. Their escape was well planned. They had some homemade weapons. One by one, the convicts overpowered two guards and eight maintenance supervisors as they returned from lunch on December 13, 2000. The convicts then changed into the maintenance workers' civilian clothes and drove a prison pickup truck to an outside gate. There they overpowered a guard who thought they were a civilian work crew. Once outside they drove a few miles to a Wal-Mart parking lot. Awaiting them were a Chevy Suburban and $300 cash, left by the father of one of the escapees and a family friend.

The desperate escapees went on a crime spree. They stole weapons, walkie-talkies, and a police scanner. Despite a massive manhunt, they eluded capture. By Christmas Eve, they were in Irving. Shortly after closing, the men drew weapons on surprised employees. They were tying them up when Irving police officer Aubrey Hawkins arrived at the scene. Officer Hawkins was killed by a hail of gunfire. He was also run over by the gang as they made their escape in a stolen Ford Explorer.

The manhunt intensified but the seven remained on the run. The break in the case came in late January. A viewer of *America's Most Wanted,* which had aired weekly reports about the seven from the time of their escape, called in to report she had seen them near her home in Woodland Park, Colorado. Police quickly surrounded a mobile home where the men were believed to be staying. One of the escapees, Larry Harper, committed suicide; the other four surrendered. Two days later, the final two escapees were apprehended at the Holiday Inn in Colorado Springs.

The six surviving escapees were returned to Dallas County, where they were each tried separately for the capital murder of Officer Hawkins. Each of the six was convicted and sentenced to death. Raul Rodriguez, Michael Rodriguez's father, was convicted for his role in providing the getaway car and received the maximum sentence of 10 years in prison.

The seven escapees, along with their ages and sentences at the time of the escape were

- **George Rivas, 30, serving 17 life sentences for aggravated robbery and kidnapping. (Sentenced to death.)**
- **Randy Halprin, 23, serving a 30-year sentence for injury to a child. (Sentenced to death.)**
- **Joseph Garcia, 29, serving a 50-year sentence for murder. (Sentenced to death.)**
- **Michael Rodriguez, 38, serving a life sentence for capital murder. (Sentenced to death.)**
- **Larry Harper, 37, serving a 50-year sentence for aggravated sexual assault. (Committed suicide.)**
- **Patrick Murphy, 39, serving a 50-year sentence for aggravated sexual assault. (Sentenced to death.)**
- **Donald Newbury, 38, serving a 99-year sentence for aggravated robbery. (Sentenced to death.)**

Officer Aubrey Hawkins is survived by a widow and a son, 9 years old at the time of his father's death.

Bail Jumping/Failure to Appear In bail jumping, a defendant fails to appear for a scheduled court appearance. If the defendant fails to appear for a Class C misdemeanor, the failure to appear is also a Class C misdemeanor. Failure to appear for other misdemeanors is a Class A misdemeanor. Failure to appear for felonies is a third-degree felony.

Taking Drugs or Alcohol into Confinement Facilities Broadly defined, it is unlawful for a person to take drugs or alcohol into any type of confinement facility. It is also unlawful for a person to take drugs onto property owned or used by the Texas Department of Criminal Justice. Violations of this section are third-degree felonies.

DISRUPTION OR OTHERWISE INAPPROPRIATE CONDUCT

Many statutes cover disruption or otherwise inappropriate conduct. Seven of these statutes are most likely to be enforced.

Disorderly Conduct The statute on disorderly conduct prohibits several types of conduct: obscene language or offensive gestures likely to incite a breach of the peace, fighting, stink bombs, window peeping, and nudity that would be offensive to others. Public discharge of a firearm or display of a deadly weapon in a way likely to alarm others is also disorderly conduct. Disorderly conduct is a Class C misdemeanor except for public firearms discharge or deadly weapon display, which are Class B misdemeanors.

40,393 arrests were made in 2003 for disorderly conduct.

Source: Texas Department of Public Safety, Crime in Texas, 2003

Riot A gathering constitutes a riot if seven or more people assemble and do at least one of the following:

- create an immediate danger of property or person injury
- interfere with a government function
- take away any person's legal right or disrupt his or her ability to engage in that right

Riot is a Class B misdemeanor or a higher degree crime equal to the most serious crime committed by any of the rioters that either furthered their purpose or that could have been anticipated.

Disrupting Meetings The statute on disrupting meetings stipulates that it is unlawful for a person to disrupt or interfere with a meeting, parade, or other gathering. The interference can be either physical or verbal. Disrupting meetings is a Class B misdemeanor.

False Alarm A person violates the law against false alarm when he or she makes a false report that would cause an emergency agency to react, would place someone in fear of serious injury, or would interfere with the lawful occupation of a place or vehicle. False alarm is a Class A misdemeanor. If the false report involves an emergency dealing with a public utility, school, or transportation, it becomes a state jail felony. A related statute makes it a Class B misdemeanor to place a silent or abuse call to a 911 emergency line.

Abuse of Corpse The abuse of corpse statute involves a person removing, disturbing, buying, or selling a human corpse. Abuse of corpse is a Class A misdemeanor.

Cruelty to Animals Broadly, the statute on cruelty to animals stipulates that it is unlawful for a person to torture, overwork, neglect, or otherwise cruelly treat animals. *Animal* does not include an uncaptured wild animal. Properly conducted scientific research is also excluded. Cruelty to animals is a Class A misdemeanor.

Dog Fighting In dog fighting, a person causes one dog to fight with another, whether or not for financial gain. This statute also applies to a person who trains dogs for this purpose, provides a place for this purpose, or attends such a fight as a spectator. Dog fighting is a state jail felony. If it is not for financial gain or the defendant only trained the dogs, it is a Class A misdemeanor. Participation as a spectator is a Class C misdemeanor.

HARASSMENT AND STALKING The harassment law deals primarily with telephone harassment, although some forms of written harassment are also covered. In 1993, the legislature added stalking to the forms of harassment.

Harassment A harasser intends to annoy, alarm, abuse, torment, or embarrass the victim. The harasser must

- call or write the victim with an obscene comment
- call or write with a threat to commit bodily injury or a felony
- falsely report serious bodily injury or death knowing that the report is false
- call anonymously or cause the victim's phone to ring repeatedly
- intentionally fail to hang up after a call
- allow someone else to use the phone for any of the above purposes

Harassment is a Class B misdemeanor.

Stalking Stalking is a form of harassment. The stalking law, ruled unconstitutional in 1996 on the grounds that it was too vague, was more precisely defined and became the first law passed by the 1997 legislature. The new law makes it illegal to repeatedly engage in conduct that threatens bodily injury, death, or property damage to the victim or the victim's family or a household member. A first conviction is a Class A misdemeanor; a second conviction is a third-degree felony.

INTOXICATION OFFENSES As of September 1, 1994, intoxication statutes dramatically increased the punishments for DWIs that cause serious bodily injury or death. *Intoxication* does not mean "drunk." The legal definition of intoxication includes a person who does not have the normal use of mental or physical faculties because of any substance in the body. This substance can be alcohol, legal or illegal drugs, any other substance, or a combination of substances. Also, intoxication means a blood alcohol concentration of 0.08 or more. To have a blood alcohol concentration of 0.08, a person of 150 pounds would have to consume about four beers or mixed drinks in one hour.

130,984 arrests were made in 2003 for public drunkenness.

Source: Texas Department of Public Safety, Crime in Texas, 2003

Driving While Intoxicated Driving while intoxicated involves a person driving or operating a motor vehicle in a public place while intoxicated. Parallel laws make it illegal to operate an aircraft or watercraft while intoxicated. This Class B misdemeanor carries a minimum punishment of 72 hours' confinement. This minimum increases to 6 days if the driver had an open container of alcohol in his or her immediate possession. A second DWI is a Class A misdemeanor with a minimum of 30 days confinement. Third and subsequent DWIs are third-degree felonies. A separate law makes driving while intoxicated, with a passenger under 15 years old in the vehicle, a state jail felony even for the first or second offense.

91,429 individuals were arrested for DWI in 2003. Of these, 10,674 were minors, too young to legally purchase alcohol.

Source: Texas Department of Public Safety, Crime in Texas, 2003

Intoxication Assault Intoxication assault, an offense newly defined as of September 1, 1994, at long last recognizes the gravity of a DWI that results in serious bodily injury. A person commits intoxication assault when driving, flying, or boating while intoxicated and by reason of that intoxication causing serious bodily injury to another person. Intoxication assault is a third-degree felony.

Before intoxication assault became the law, such cases had to be prosecuted as DWIs. Even in situations where one or more victims were left paralyzed for life, the maximum punishment was a misdemeanor jail sentence. The intoxication assault statute fosters a greater recognition of the horrendous effect this crime can have on victims.

Intoxication Manslaughter A person drives, flies, or boats while intoxicated and by reason of that intoxication causes the death of another person. As part of the tougher 1994 laws against DWI, the legislature created intoxication manslaughter as a renamed version of involuntary manslaughter involving DWI. Under the old law, involuntary manslaughter involving DWI was a third-degree felony; intoxication manslaughter is second-degree felony.

Failure to Stop and Render Aid A person who operates a motor vehicle in an accident involving death or injury has a duty to stop the vehicle and provide reasonable assistance such as notifying emergency personnel. Failure to stop and render aid is a felony punishable by

- confinement in prison for up to 5 years
- confinement in a county jail for up to 1 year
- a fine of up to $5,000
- both the fine and the confinement

Other Offenses There are statutes against both public intoxication and consumption or possession of an alcoholic beverage in a motor vehicle. A publicly intoxicated person appears in a public place sufficiently intoxicated to endanger either self or another person. Consumption or possession of an alcoholic beverage in a motor vehicle—a person driving in public while consuming an alcoholic beverage—is also unlawful. Both of these crimes are Class C misdemeanors.

MAD MOTHERS . . . AND FATHERS, BROTHERS, SISTERS, ETC.

On May 3, 1980, thirteen-year-old Cari Lightner was killed by a drunk driver while she walked to a church carnival near her home in Fair Oaks, California. The drunk driver had a long history of intoxication arrests. In fact, he had been released on bond the previous week for hit-and-run drunk driving. Cari's mother, Candy, was told by police that it was unlikely

the driver would do any time behind bars because, after all, drunk driving was just one of those things. Candy refused to accept the status quo and began a one-woman crusade to strengthen drunk driving laws. Her efforts ultimately led to the founding of Mothers Against Drunk Driving (MADD). Cari's killer, Clarence Busch, was convicted and served 21 months in jail.

Since then MADD has mushroomed into a nationwide organization with some 350 affiliates and a million supporters. There are even international affiliates in Canada, New Zealand, Australia, Ireland, Sweden, and Great Britain. Due to MADD, all 50 states have toughened their drunk driving laws. A nonstop barrage of public awareness and community education programs has helped change public attitudes. MADD staff and volunteers also provide assistance and support to victims and their families.

MADD has succeeded. Drunk driving is no longer acceptable; fewer people do it. Nationwide, the drunk driving slaughter in 1982 included 25,165 fatalities and was expected to rise. Instead, the number declined to 17,461 in 1993 and has remained at that lower level for the past decade. Literally tens of thousands of Americans are alive today because of anti–drunk driving initiatives spearheaded by MADD.

PUBLIC INDECENCY

Prostitution A prostitute, male or female, engages in sexual conduct for a fee. Also, a person solicits such conduct in a public place. Both the prostitute and the customer are equally guilty of the offense. Prostitution is a Class B misdemeanor. A second conviction is a Class A misdemeanor.

6,508 arrests occurred in 2003 for prostitution and related offenses.

Source: Texas Department of Public Safety, Crime in Texas, 2003

Promotion of Prostitution The promotion of prostitution statute stipulates that it is unlawful for a person other than the prostitute to either receive part of the proceeds of the prostitution or solicit business for the prostitute. Promotion of prostitution is a Class A misdemeanor.

Aggravated Promotion of Prostitution Promotion of prostitution is aggravated if a person manages or has a financial interest in two or more prostitutes. Aggravated promotion is a third-degree felony.

Compelling Prostitution In the offense of compelling prostitution, a person

- causes another to commit prostitution by threat or fraud
- causes a child younger than 17 to commit prostitution

Compelling prostitution is a second-degree felony.

Obscenity What is obscene? Many people agree with U.S. Supreme Court Justice Potter Stewart, who indicated that obscenity may be difficult to define but "I know it when I see it." Nonetheless, Texas law has three requirements:

- An average person, using contemporary community standards, must find that the material as a whole appeals to prurient sexual interests.
- The material must describe or depict sexual or excretory acts.
- Viewed as a whole, the material must lack serious literary, artistic, political, or scientific value.

Promotion, selling, or other distribution of obscene material is a Class A misdemeanor. Wholesale promotion or distribution for resale purposes is a state jail felony.

Sale, Distribution, or Display of Harmful Material to a Minor The law against the sale, distribution, or display of harmful material to a minor is similar to the obscenity law except that it specifies the involvement of a minor, and *harmful* is more broadly defined than is *obscenity*. A minor is a child under 18. Harmful material

- appeals to the prurient interest of a minor in sex, nudity, or excretion
- patently offends the adult community's standards for what is suitable for minors
- has no redeeming social value for minors

The sale, distribution, exhibition, or reckless display of harmful material to a minor is a Class A misdemeanor. If the defendant hires or otherwise uses a minor to commit this crime, it is a third-degree felony.

Sexual Performance by a Child Under the statute on sexual performance by a child, it is unlawful for a person to employ or otherwise allow a child under 18 to engage in a sexual performance or sexual conduct. A parent or guardian who consents to such conduct is also guilty. Employing or permitting sexual performance by a child is a second-degree felony, unless the defendant produced or promoted the sexual performance, in which case it is a third-degree felony.

Employment Harmful to Children Employment harmful to children involves a person employing a child under 18 in a sexually oriented business such as a massage parlor, or in a place where the child works nude or a female child works topless. This crime is a Class A misdemeanor.

Child Pornography A child pornographer possesses or distributes a film image of a child under 18 engaging in sexual conduct. *Film image* includes photographs, negatives, and videotapes. Child pornography is a third-degree felony.

WEAPONS OFFENSES

Unlawfully Carrying a Weapon In the crime of unlawfully carrying a weapon, a person carries a handgun, an illegal knife, or a club. A knife is illegal if its blade is more than 5½ inches.

The many exceptions to this law include

- military personnel
- peace officers
- possession on your own premises
- traveling
- hunting, fishing, or other sports activities which commonly use that weapon
- uniformed security officers traveling to or engaged in their work

11,904 arrests occurred in 2003 for weapons offenses.

Source: Texas Department of Public Safety, Crime in Texas, 2003

Beginning January 1, 1996, it became possible to obtain a license to carry a concealed handgun in public. A person has to have been a Texas resident for at least six months, be 21 years of age, and not have had a felony conviction. Numerous other requirements prohibit licenses for those with certain misdemeanor or juvenile convictions, those with chemical dependency or mental problems, and those who are subjects of protective orders, are delinquent on child support or state tax payments, or are defaulters on student loans. Those eligible for a license must take a 10- to 15-hour handgun proficiency course, provide fingerprints and biographical data, and pay a nonrefundable fee of $140 ($70 for indigents and those over 60). A license is good for four years.

Even with a license, it is a Class A misdemeanor for the licensed person to carry the handgun into a hospital, a nursing home, most sporting events, an amusement park, a church, a government meeting —or any place when the person is intoxicated. It is a third-degree felony for the licensed person to carry the handgun into a bar, jail, or prison. Unlawfully carrying a weapon is a Class A misdemeanor. If the weapon is carried into a place where alcoholic beverages are sold, this crime is a third-degree felony.

Prohibited Places Citizens are prohibited by law from possessing weapons in certain places. It is unlawful for a person to possess any weapon, from a firearm to brass knuckles, at

- schools (public or private) and on school buses
- polling places
- courts or court offices
- racetracks
- secure portions of an airport

Exceptions are limited to military personnel, law enforcement personnel, and certain uniformed security guards. Carrying a weapon in a prohibited place is a third-degree felony.

Unlawful Possession of a Firearm by a Felon It is unlawful for a felon to possess a firearm; that is, for a person convicted of a felony to possess any type of firearm at any place for any purpose. Five years after the person has been released from parole or probation supervision, he or she may possess a firearm at home only.

> **63%** **of murders are committed with a firearm, usually a handgun.**
>
> *Source: Texas Department of Public Safety*

Prohibited Weapons Possession of certain weapons is prohibited by law:

- an explosive weapon
- a machine gun

- a short-barrel firearm
- a firearm silencer
- a switchblade
- brass knuckles
- armor-piercing ammunition
- chemical-dispensing device
- a zip gun

Exceptions are made for certain military and law enforcement personnel. There is also an exception for small, commercially available mace or pepper-type dispensers used for personal protection, as well as for antique or curio items and items registered under the National Firearms Act. Possession of a switchblade or brass knuckles is a Class A misdemeanor. Possession of all other weapons is a third-degree felony. Possession of the components of an explosive weapon with intent to combine them is also a third-degree felony.

ILLEGAL GAMBLING Private gambling between individuals where the benefit to any participant is limited to personal winnings is legal in Texas. Other forms of gambling are generally illegal; however, bingo, raffles, the lottery, and horse and dog racing are specifically authorized under certain rules and licensing requirements.

Gambling It is illegal for a person to place bets on an event such as a ball game, dice, or card game. Gambling under such circumstances is a Class C misdemeanor.

466 arrests occurred in 2003 for gambling offenses.

Source: Texas Department of Public Safety, Crime in Texas, 2003

Other Offenses Several other gambling-related activities are illegal in Texas:

- promoting gambling—book making
- keeping a gambling place—permitting another to use real estate or a vehicle for illegal gambling
- communicating gambling information—furthering illegal gambling by communicating information about bets or odds
- possessing gambling equipment—possession of gambling devices, equipment, or paraphernalia with intent to further gambling

All of these offenses are Class A misdemeanors.

ORGANIZED CRIME Texas, fortunately, was spared most of the activities of La Cosa Nostra and other traditional organized crime families. We do, however, have smaller groups that collaborate to commit crimes such as burglary or drug dealing. In recent years, organized crime laws have been used against youth gangs.

Engaging in Organized Criminal Activity The crime of engaging in organized criminal activity involves three or more people who collaborate on certain criminal activities. It is not necessary for all the members to know each other. Some of them may operate on different levels, such as those in a wholesale/retail relationship. The criminal activity must include one of several dozen named offenses, which include all violent offenses and most drug offenses, theft, gambling, and obscenity. Since 1993, additions of burglary of a motor vehicle, unauthorized use of a motor vehicle, deadly conduct, and Class A misdemeanor assault make it easier to apply this statute to youth gangs.

Engaging in organized criminal activity is classified as one punishment level more serious than the most serious crime committed by the group. If the defendants were only a part of the conspiracy and did not actually commit the crime, they are punished on the same level as if they had committed the crime.

Money Laundering In the crime of money laundering, a person spends, receives, transports, or invests funds which are the proceeds from a felony offense. Punishment depends on the amount of money involved: $3,000 up to $20,000 is a third-degree felony; $20,000 up to $100,000 is a second-degree felony; $100,000 or more is a first-degree felony.

DRUG CRIMES The Texas Controlled Substances Act is part of the Health and Safety Code rather than the Penal Code. The Controlled Substances Act defines which drugs are illegal and sets punishment ranges based upon the harmfulness and quantity of the drug.

Each penalty group contains the scientific names of numerous drugs with definitions broad enough to prevent chemists from making legal drugs by slightly altering the chemical make-up. Marijuana has its own classification.

LOST WAR?

The media has popularized the myth that the War on Drugs has been lost. In fact, drug usage steadily increased during the 1970s and peaked in the early- to mid-1980s. National attention then focused on the issue, which led to the creation of a

cabinet-level "drug czar" in Washington, a massive multi-faceted drug education program that reached every school child, and tougher enforcement of drug laws. This extraordinary effort produced a dramatic decline in drug usage. For example, active drug use (last 30 days) among young adults (18- to 25-year-olds) peaked at 37% in 1979 and decreased to 13% in 1992. Similarly, past-year cocaine usage by high school seniors peaked at 13% in 1985 and fell to 3% by 1993. There were some relatively small increases in drug usage during the mid-1990s, but drug usage has remained relatively constant since then. Overall, the situation is much improved from the peak years in the 1970s. Some illustrative examples of drug usage declines are:

- **Active drug usage (last 30 days) among 18- to 25-year-olds peaked at 37% in 1979 and decreased to 19% in 2001.**
- **Active marijuana usage (last 30 days) among high school seniors peaked at 37% in 1979 and decreased to 25% in 2001.**
- **Active cocaine usage (last 30 days) by 18- to 25-year-olds peaked at 9.9% in 1985 and decreased to 1.9% in 2001.**

These basic trends have held true for all drugs and all age groups. Although the collection of data and reporting of these statistics lags several years behind, first reports indicate that drug use was declining across the board in 2002 and 2003.

Possession Possession means that a person has custody or control of the substance. Actual physical possession is not required. A person can possess a substance found in his or her home or car even though he or she is miles away.

Delivery A person engaging in delivery transfers a substance to another person. It is not necessary to prove a sale. Delivery includes constructive transfers; that is, instructing someone else to make the delivery or instructing the buyer to pick the substance up at an unoccupied location such as a post office box. Delivery also includes offers to sell drugs. Possession of a drug with intent to deliver (except marijuana) is punished the same as a delivery.

Manufacture A person who manufactures produces drugs. This includes the chemist who actually makes the drugs, but it also includes anyone who packages or repackages the drugs. Marijuana growing is specifically excluded from this definition.

Penalty Groups Each group of illegal drugs is classified in a penalty group. Group I contains nearly all hard drugs: cocaine, heroin,

LSD (lysergic acid diethylamide), methamphetamine, Ecstasy, and also the "date rape" drug Rohypnol. Penalty Group II includes psilocybin, usually in the form of hallucinogenic mushrooms, and hashish. Penalty Group III includes many prescription drugs, such as Valium (diazepam) and Percodan (oxycodone). Penalty Group IV contains a shorter listing of drugs, such as prescription cough medicine containing codeine.

DRUG PRICES

The types of drugs abused and the prices of drugs fluctuate. A recent check with a police drug lab indicates that the three most often seized drugs are marijuana, cocaine (both crack and powdered) and Ecstasy. Methamphetamine is another drug frequently seized. LSD and heroin, while still seen, are currently not very popular.

How much do illegal drugs cost? Most of these substances are usually sold by the gram, ounce, or pound. (A gram is about the weight of an individual packet of artificial sweetener.)

Cocaine	
gram	**$60**
ounce	**$600**
pound	**$9,000**
Marijuana	
ounce	**$60**
pound	**$500**
Ecstasy	
1 hit	**$25**

Punishment Classifications The punishment range for Penalty Group I offenses is:

Possession:

less than 1 gram—state jail felony (probation is mandatory for first offenses)

1 gram to less than 4 grams—third-degree felony

4 grams to less than 200 grams—second-degree felony

200 grams to less than 400 grams—first-degree felony

400 grams or more—10 years to life plus a fine up to $100,000

Manufacture or delivery:

less than 1 gram—state jail felony

1 gram to less than 4 grams—second-degree felony

4 grams to less than 200 grams—first-degree felony

200 grams to less than 400 grams—10 years to life plus a fine up to $100,000

400 grams or more—15 years to life plus a fine up to $250,000

Punishment ranges for manufacture and delivery of drugs in Penalty Groups II, III, and IV are only slightly less harsh than those for drugs in Penalty Group I. Any manufacture or delivery is a felony and any offense involving 400 grams or more carries a potential life sentence. Punishment ranges for possession of drugs in Penalty Groups II, III, and IV vary more than the delivery/manufacture ranges. Possession of Penalty Group II substances is always a felony. However, possession of less than 28 grams of a Penalty Group III or IV substance is a misdemeanor. Possession of large quantities (400 grams or more) of these drugs carries a potential life sentence.

To put these weights into perspective, one gram is the size of an individual serving of the kind of artificial sweetener found in pink or blue packages at restaurants. Although prices fluctuate, a gram of cocaine costs roughly $60. Four hundred grams is slightly less than one pound. Four hundred grams of cocaine would cost roughly $9,000.

LSD classifications are slightly different from other major drugs since LSD is used and sold by "hits," or abuse units. The Texas Legislature has determined that 20 abuse units equals 1 gram of the other Penalty Group I substances and set up a punishment scale accordingly. Thus, possession of less than 20 abuse units of LSD is a state jail felony (the same as possession of less than 1 gram of cocaine), while possession of 20–79 abuse units is a third degree felony (the same as possession of from 1 to less than 4 grams of cocaine).

Marijuana Since marijuana quantities differ from those of other drugs, they have their own classification system. There is no separate offense for manufacture or possession with intent to deliver.

Possession:

2 oz. or less—Class B misdemeanor

more than 2 oz. to 4 oz.—Class A misdemeanor

more than 4 oz. to 5 lbs.—state jail felony (if less than 1 lb., probation is mandatory for first offense)

more than 5 lbs. to 50 lbs.—third-degree felony

more than 50 lbs. to 2,000 lbs.—second-degree felony

more than 2,000 lbs.—5 years to life and a fine not to exceed $50,000

Delivery:

¼ oz. or less (no payment)—Class B misdemeanor

¼ oz. or less (with payment)—Class A misdemeanor

more than ¼ oz. to 5 lbs.—state jail felony

more than 5 lbs. to 50 lbs.—second-degree felony

more than 50 lbs. to 2,000 lbs.—first-degree felony

more than 2,000 lbs.—10 years to life and a fine not to exceed $100,000

Illegal Expenditure or Investment A person spends money to further a major drug crime or spends profits derived from a major drug crime. Marijuana offenses of 50 lbs. or less are the only major offenses excluded. Illegal expenditure or investment is a first-degree felony.

Fraud In drug fraud, a person fraudulently obtains prescription drugs. The classification of offenses under this section ranges from Class A misdemeanors to second-degree felonies.

Triplicate Prescriptions The triplicate prescription program has greatly reduced abuse of prescription drugs. The most abused drugs, such as pain killers, can be prescribed only on special triplicate forms that identify the physician, the pharmacy, and the patient. Both the physician and the pharmacist must keep a copy of the prescription for two years. The third copy goes to the Department of Public Safety. The Department of Public Safety can then determine whether a physician is writing an unusually high number of prescriptions or whether a patient is filling multiple prescriptions.

PREVENTION THAT WORKS

D.A.R.E. (Drug Abuse Resistance Education) is the largest, most successful drug education program in the country. In D.A.R.E., an experienced uniformed law enforcement officer works in conjunction with a classroom teacher to teach 17 weekly lessons to a class of fifth or sixth graders.

D.A.R.E. is taught as a partnership of community, parents, schools, and law enforcement. Law enforcement officers and educators provide both drug education and resistance techniques to kids before they go to middle school or junior high.

We want kids to recognize and resist both direct and indirect pressures that would influence them to experiment with tobacco, alcohol, inhalants, or other drugs or to engage in violence or gang activity.

D.A.R.E. was developed in 1984 by the Los Angeles school system and police department. It soon began to spread throughout the nation. In 1988 it was cited as a model program by the White House Conference for a Drug Free America. Today, it is offered in all 50 states and it has tens of millions of graduates. In Texas, 900 active D.A.R.E. officers teach the program throughout the state.

At the conclusion of the D.A.R.E. program, students write an essay entitled "Taking a Stand," which articulates their commitment to be drug-free and to avoid violence. At graduation, they receive a T-shirt with the red D.A.R.E. logo.

If you don't have a child or grandchild who has gone through D.A.R.E., you may wonder what the T-shirt or the bumper sticker with the red D.A.R.E. logo means. It represents one of the millions of kids who want a better, drug-free world. If you see a child wearing such a T-shirt, please go up and give that kid a hearty congratulations.

Delivery of a Controlled Substance or Marijuana to a Minor Texas law prohibits delivery of a controlled substance or marijuana to a minor—that is, delivery of any quantity of marijuana or a Penalty Group I, II, or III substance to a person 17 or younger or a student enrolled in an elementary or secondary school. This law excludes persons under 18 or persons under 21 who deliver less than ¼ ounce of marijuana without receiving payment. Delivery of a controlled substance or marijuana to a minor is a second-degree felony.

Drug-Free Zones In an effort to keep drugs out of the schools, the legislature has designated as drug-free zones the areas within 1,000 feet of a school (including colleges and universities) or a playground and within 300 feet of a youth center, public swimming pool, or video arcade. If delivery occurs in this zone, the minimum term of confinement and the maximum fine are doubled.

Inhalants Broadly speaking, it is unlawful for a person to inhale an otherwise legal substance to create a high feeling or hallucination effect on the mind. Inhalants, including spray paints, white-out, and gasoline additives, are deadly and highly addictive. Because of their legal uses, they are difficult to control. The legislature created two regulatory systems for these substances.

The first system requires permits for stores to sell abusable glues and aerosol paints. Such permits must be displayed. Delivering such substances to a minor younger than 18 is a state jail felony. Exceptions are made for parents letting a child use such a product for its proper purpose under the parents' supervision and for employees who are shown an apparently valid driver's license indicating that the buyer is at least 18 years old. Possession or use of an inhalant for improper purposes is a Class B misdemeanor.

The second system regulates volatile chemicals, most of which are solvents or gasoline additives. Gasoline is specifically exempted. Delivering any volatile chemical to a person under 18 is a Class B misdemeanor. Exceptions are made for employees who are shown an apparently valid driver's license and for physicians, dentists, and other professionals with legitimate reasons to give such substances to minors.

This chapter detailed the various criminal laws and their punishments. But punishment ranges by themselves have little meaning without an understanding of probation, prison, and parole. The next chapter provides a detailed explanation of how each of these three systems works.

CHAPTER 4

CRIMINAL PUNISHMENTS

As a society, we sentence criminals for three reasons:

1. *Punishment,* which most often means a prison sentence, is a bad consequence for a bad act.
2. *Rehabilitation,* which most often involves probation, refers to formal education, vocational training, and substance abuse programs designed to change a criminal into a productive member of society.
3. *Deterrence* refers to punishment intended to keep offenders from committing more crimes, usually by putting them into prison. The threat of imprisonment also scares others into not committing crimes.

Those who debate these issues—whether over coffee or on the editorial page—generally belong to the pro-punishment group or the pro-rehabilitation group. I have read or heard arguments that prison is good, that prison is bad, that prison is too expensive, and that prison coddles criminals. I have also read or heard arguments that probation is good, bad, too expensive, or that it coddles criminals.

In practice, as a society we generally agree that 17-year-old nonviolent offenders should get some type of probation. Habitual violent offenders, we agree, should be locked up. Beyond that, opinions vary sharply. However, from my experience with the criminal justice system, it is obvious that when Texas juries learn about real crimes, they are able to reach a consensus—a consensus that frequently involves a lengthy prison sentence.

As a prosecutor and now as a judge, I have to deal with reality, not theory. I have to craft sentences and help develop a system that can punish, rehabilitate, and deter. As district attorney, my office sought prison sentences for violent offenders, child molesters, drug dealers, house burglars, and repeat offenders. I also worked for the creation of a model drug treatment center, a community service restitution program, and drug testing for nearly all probationers.

As you read this chapter, you will see that the Texas sentencing system is much more complicated than is widely assumed in the news media. Probation can, in fact, involve a fair amount of punishment—up to a year of confinement in some cases. Further, parole eligibility is a good deal tougher than it was a few years ago. Texas has the country's largest prison system, with lots of maximum security beds.

Before I begin discussing punishment, I'd like to share with you a jury argument that I used to give and current prosecutors still use: "When you go home tonight, you will lock yourselves in your house. You will check to see that you locked your windows, that your deadbolted doors are secure. Perhaps you will even turn on a security system. There is something very wrong with a society where the good people are locked up while the criminals are running free on the street."

As a society, we need to understand that we have a right to protect ourselves. Yes, prisons are terrible places. We shouldn't sugarcoat this fact. They are metal and concrete cages where we lock up human beings. They are also very necessary. As long as people break the law, society has a right—in fact, a duty—to fill its prisons.

I have heard many arguments used against new prison construction. Words like *mercy, enlightenment,* and *economics*. However well meant the sentiments behind the terms are, though, they lead to unacceptable crime rates, to the Kenneth McDuffs being released, and to the good citizens locking themselves up each night.

Our government's first obligation is the protection of its citizens. As a society, we don't need to accept locked doors, burglar alarms, and fear as inevitable. We need to demand from our legislators, judges, prosecutors, and law enforcement officials a system that first and foremost keeps us safe.

TYPES OF PUNISHMENT As recently as 1980, Texas had only three felony punishment options: prison, probation, or parole. The main condition for probation and parole was to avoid arrest for another crime; little else was required. Probation and parole seldom meant punishment or rehabilitation. Since then, punishment options have expanded greatly. Residential options—from restitution centers to boot camps—were unheard of a few years ago. Conditions of probation have also changed dramatically. Restitution to victims, drug rehabilitation programs, community service work, and jail sentences are standard parts of many probated sentences. Probation, at least for first offenders with nonviolent crimes, no longer necessarily means getting off easy for a crime. In fact, some defendants would rather go to prison than be supervised on probation.

COMMUNITY SUPERVISION (PROBATION) Commonly referred to as "probation," this system supervises the conduct of convicted criminals. The judge suspends their sentences as long as they follow certain written requirements.

Probation officers who work for a local Community Supervision and Corrections Department (CSCD) supervise the probationers. The period of supervision may be up to 10 calendar years. The conditions of probation may include confinement in a rehabilitation center. Upon violating a condition of probation, the criminal can be confined in prison or a state jail. Even if the judge decides not to send the criminal to prison, he or she will usually make the conditions of probation more severe.

270,788 convicted criminals are on community supervision in Texas. Of these, 158,490 were convicted for felony crimes and 112,298 for misdemeanors.

Source: Texas Department of Criminal Justice, Community Justice Assistance Division

ELIGIBILITY Probation can be granted by judges or juries under specified circumstances. Judges may grant probation to any defendant whose sentence does not exceed 10 years. Judges may not grant probation to a defendant convicted of murder, capital murder, indecency with a child by contact, aggravated kidnapping, sexual assault, aggravated sexual assault, aggravated robbery, or any crime during which a deadly weapon was used or exhibited.

Juries may grant probation only if the defendant files a sworn application stating that they have no prior felony convictions. The defendant must also prove this fact. Again, the sentence must not exceed 10 years, but juries may grant probation for any offense. A judge must follow a jury's recommendation for probation. However, the judge sets the exact conditions of probation.

BASIC CONDITIONS Judges may impose any reasonable condition "to protect or restore the community, protect or restore the victim, or punish, rehabilitate, or reform the defendant." The law sets out 23 basic reasonable conditions. Judges impose 10 of these on nearly every probationer. The probationer shall

- Commit no offense against the law.
- Avoid injurious or vicious habits.
- Avoid disreputable or harmful persons or places.
- Report to a probation officer weekly or monthly.
- Permit a probation officer to visit at home or elsewhere.
- Work at suitable employment.
- Pay any fine.
- Support any dependents.
- Remain in the county of conviction. The probation officer will usually require written permits for travel.
- Perform community service work.

Judges impose the other 13 conditions when applicable and appropriate for monitoring, rehabilitation, and payment of fees. Examples:

- drug and alcohol tests
- electronic monitors
- confinement in a community corrections facility
- substance abuse counseling
- reimbursement (court-appointed lawyers, the Crime Victims' Compensation Fund, victim counseling or HIV testing, costs for testing or disposing of drugs)

$47,627,037 **was paid by probationers to their victims in 2003 as restitution for their crimes.**

Source: Texas Department of Criminal Justice, Community Justice Assistance Division

OTHER CONDITIONS Commonly, judges add one or more specific conditions tailored to the individual case. The law requires judges either to order full financial restitution or to give reasons for not ordering it.

Judges must also order a probationer to become sufficiently literate to test at an educational level equivalent to at least the sixth grade. Most judges go beyond that minimum and require a high school dropout to get a GED and an unemployed or underemployed probationer to get job training.

Judges may require additional education or job training or treatment for alcohol abuse, substance abuse, or psychological problems. For example, I frequently require mandatory attendance at a set number of Alcoholics Anonymous meetings per week. Psychological treatment may range from individual therapy to group programs for everyone from hot check writers to spouse batterers to child molesters.

CREATIVE SENTENCING

Sentencing judges can craft unique conditions for probation or other sentences. This process is called "creative sentencing." For example, some judges routinely make probationers write letters of apology to their victims or make DWI defendants place a warning sticker on their car bumpers.

I recently sentenced a woman who stole money from her son's elementary school PTA to a probated sentence that included 300 hours of washing school buses and hand writing 700 notes of apology—one to each of the students at the school. Also, I ordered a juvenile who "keyed" a teacher's car to write the teacher a letter of apology and to get a part-time job and pay $1,000 restitution.

Former Houston District Judge Ted Poe is perhaps the most well known of these creative judges.

- **A hair salon owner was convicted of criminal mischief by driving his car through a neighbor's yard. Judge Poe ordered the defendant to move, to make restitution, and to cut hair at state schools for the blind and retarded every Saturday for the five years of his probation.**
- **A piano teacher was convicted of sexually assaulting his young pupils. Judge Poe ordered him to donate his $12,000 piano to a local children's home and post a sign on his door warning young people to stay away. Judge Poe also ordered him not to play the piano for the 10 years of his probation.**
- **A drunk driver killed a young couple and seriously injured their two children. Judge Poe ordered him to keep a photograph of his victims on the wall of his jail cell.**

LIMITATIONS ON CONDITIONS Other than the general requirement that conditions of probation be reasonable, judges can order conditions as they see fit. However, the law limits financial conditions to fines, court costs, victim restitution, rehabilitation programs, fees and reimbursements for prosecution and supervision, and a $50 one-time payment to a Crime Stoppers program.

COMMUNITY SERVICE Community service work is done for nonprofit organizations or government agencies. It can include anything from picking up trash to providing skilled labor on a construction project. Community service work is a required condition of any probation. The judge can exempt probationers from this requirement only for good cause, such as mental or physical inability or confinement in a substance abuse punishment facility.

The judge gives a length of community service work within ranges set by the legislature.

First-degree felony: 320–1000 hours

Second-degree felony: 240–800 hours

Third-degree felony: 160–600 hours

State jail felony: 120–400 hours

Class A misdemeanor: 80–200 hours

Class B misdemeanor: 24–100 hours

JAIL The judge can also order confinement in a county jail as a condition of probation:

- up to 30 days for misdemeanors
- up to 180 days for felonies

COMMUNITY CORRECTIONS FACILITIES Judges can require probationers to live in one of six types of Community Corrections Facilities (CCFs). Working probationers pay for their room and board.

Restitution Centers, Court Residential Treatment Facilities, and Substance Abuse Treatment Facilities Unlike jails or prisons, restitution centers, court residential treatment facilities, and substance abuse treatment facilities are not secure facilities. Even though the probationer must live there, these facilities have no armed guards or perimeter fences. All, however, provide highly structured living arrangements. Residents of restitution centers have outside jobs to repay victims and support their dependents in addition to paying room and board. Treatment facilities offer substance abuse treatment, education, and job training programs.

Boot Camps In secure facilities called "boot camps," probationers get military-style discipline and rigorous work and exercise. Local boot camps generally have longer programs than state boot camps (see below).

Facilities for Probationers with Mental Illness or Other Disability Facilities for those with mental illness or disability provide structured living and treatment. Texas has no such facilities; those who qualify go to private facilities contracted by the local Community Supervision and Corrections Department.

Intermediate Sanction Facilities Intermediate sanction facilities are similar to county jails. They were designed to ensure that probationers could be incarcerated for some period of time despite overcrowded local jails. These intermediate facilities incarcerate only probationers. A typical incarceration period would be for several months.

REVOCATION OF PROBATION If a probationer violates a judge's condition, the prosecutor may file a motion to revoke the probation. The motion sets out the specific condition that the probationer violated. The judge who originally sentenced the probationer hears the motion and issues an arrest warrant if appropriate. Arrested violators can be jailed without bond until a hearing.

At the hearing, the prosecutor must prove a violated condition by a preponderance of the evidence. This standard is easier to meet than the normal proof beyond a reasonable doubt required in criminal cases. Violators have the right to a lawyer and to call and cross-examine witnesses. They do not have the right to a jury trial. The judge can leave the violator on probation, revoke the probation, or add any new conditions from those allowable for the original probation.

TERMINATION Unless a judge revokes a probation, the probationer completes the full term of the probation. There is no good-time credit for probation. A judge can also end a probation after the offender has served the lesser of one third of the term or two years. Early termination does not apply to intoxication or sex offenses or to state jail felonies.

DEFERRED ADJUDICATION Deferred adjudication is a form of probation in which defendants are not actually convicted of a crime. After a plea of guilty or no contest, only a judge, not a jury, may defer a finding of guilt and place defendants on probation. The conditions are identical to those of any other probation. A felony may be deferred for up to 10 years. A misdemeanor may be deferred for up to 2 years.

An advantage of deferred adjudication is that it lets defendants keep a clean record. They have technically not been convicted of a crime. A disadvantage is that deferred adjudication can be revoked, just like any probation. Defendants can then be sentenced to any number of years that the offense carries, including life in prison for a first-degree felony. If defendants successfully complete their period of deferred adjudication, their criminal record remains clear. However, if they later are charged with another offense, the prior deferred adjudication can be used as evidence against them.

COMMUNITY SUPERVISION AND CORRECTIONS DEPARTMENT Texas' 121 Community Supervision and Corrections Departments (CSCDs) employ 3,325 probation officers to supervise Texas probationers. A district judge hires the CSCD director, who hires officers and staff. These CSCDs are funded by the state and by a fee—up to $60 per month—assessed each probationer.

SUBSTANCE ABUSE FELONY PUNISHMENT FACILITY Texas has made a major commitment to treating offenders' drug and alcohol problems. The cornerstone of this commitment is the Substance Abuse Felony Punishment Facility (SAFPF). The system currently operates more than 3,000 of these treatment beds. To be eligible, offenders must

- be on probation or deferred adjudication
- not be on probation for indecency with a child, sexual assault, or aggravated sexual assault
- have committed an offense to which substance abuse contributed significantly
- be suitable for treatment (e.g., no outstanding criminal charges, physical and mental ability to complete the program, no need for immediate detoxification)

The 12-step treatment at an SAFPF includes an individualized program, individual and group therapy, and education and life-skills training. The staff develops an aftercare program that will be a condition of probation. The facility also prepares residents for reentry onto probation.

SHOCK PROBATION Judges may sentence defendants to prison and then, within 180 days of their arrival at the prison, order them returned to the local community on probation. To be eligible for shock probation, the defendants must be otherwise eligible for probation and must never before have been confined in any prison. Similar provisions apply to misdemeanors. Judges may release a defendant onto probation during the first 180 days of their jail sentences. For misdemeanors, there is no limitation regarding prior jail or prison sentences.

SPECIAL CONDITIONS FOR INTOXICATION OFFENSES Certain intoxication offenses require confinement as a condition of probation. Second convictions for driving, flying, or boating while intoxicated require 72 hours of continuous confinement. Third or subsequent convictions require 10 days. Intoxication assault requires 30 days, and intoxication manslaughter requires at least 120 days.

Judges may require that probationers pay for and install ignition interlock devices on their vehicles; if such a device detects alcohol on the operator's breath, it will not allow the vehicle to start. This requirement is mandatory for third-offense DWI and for intoxication manslaughter.

Judges must require defendants convicted of an intoxication offense to attend an alcohol education course. This course must be completed within the first 180 days of probation. Judges can extend this time to the first year of probation. Failure to complete this course results in a mandatory driver's license suspension.

Conviction for an intoxication offense includes an automatic driver's license suspension. These suspensions range from 90 days to 2 years, depending on the offense, the number of prior convictions, and whether the defendant is younger than 21.

STATE BOOT CAMP The state boot camps are a form of shock probation. Operating at state prisons, they offer military-style discipline and vigorous labor. To be eligible, defendants must be felons who are

- eligible for probation
- between 17 and 25
- physically and mentally fit

After defendants have been at the state boot camp from 75 to 90 days, judges can return them to the community and release them on probation. The state boot camp is not available for those convicted of state jail felonies.

INSTITUTIONAL DIVISION The state prison system is officially known as the Institutional Division of the Texas Department of Criminal Justice. It is headquartered in Huntsville. The Institutional Division is run by the Texas Board of Criminal Justice, a nine-member commission. The members, appointed by the governor and approved by the Texas senate, are nonsalaried. They meet approximately four times a year.

The board hires the executive director of the Department of Criminal Justice and the director of the Institutional Division.

THE RUIZ PRISON LAWSUIT

In 1972, inmate David Ruiz filed a handwritten lawsuit against the state prison system. His lawsuit was combined with dozens of other such inmate suits and tried in 1985. After a long, bitter trial, Federal Judge William Wayne Justice found Texas ran an unconstitutionally brutal and overcrowded prison system. After the trial, the State of Texas and the inmates entered into an agreement called a Consent Decree. The Consent Decree gave the federal government unprecedented power over the state system and required the state to meet specific requirements in areas such as programs, recreation, health care, and the feeding and clothing of inmates. The decree also required Texas to leave 5% of its prison beds (at that time roughly 2,000 beds) empty every night.

Following the Consent Decree, Texas prisons were some of the world's least crowded, but tens of thousands of inmates were packed into local county jails not affected by the prison lawsuit. Meanwhile, parole and crime rates soared.

Finally, in late 1992, the lawsuit ended with a Final Judgment returning control of the system to state officials and eliminating the requirement of keeping 5% of prison beds empty.

What became of David Ruiz? He was paroled from prison in 1981, continued to commit crimes, and ultimately was convicted of robbery and aggravated perjury. He currently serves his life sentence in an out-of-state federal prison. His first parole eligibility will be in 2005, when he is 63 years old.

SYSTEM SIZE AND GROWTH The Institutional Division is undergoing dramatic growth. In 1991, it held approximately 38,000 inmates at 40 units. By the end of 1997, dozens of additional new units had been built. Today, the system has been completed and can hold approximately 152,000 inmates at more than 100 separate units.

These prison units, spread throughout Texas, include standard maximum security prisons, trusty camps, boot camps, detention centers, and pre-parole transfer facilities. Texas also has more specialized units, such as the acute-care hospital in Galveston. Other specialized units house less seriously ill inmates, those with mental problems, and those awaiting parole.

CLASSIFICATION At a diagnostic unit, new inmates are classified into one of seven groups on the basis of age, prior criminal history, and custody level (maximum to minimum). Males go to the diagnostic unit near Huntsville; females go to the Gatesville unit. They spend about three weeks at these units before transfer to their permanent units. Generally, young first offenders go to different units than older, repeat offenders. The classification categories are

First offender: 17–21 years old

First offender: 22–25 years old

First offender: 26 or more years old

Repeat offender: 17–21 years old

Repeat offender: 22–25 years old

Repeat offender: 26 or more years old

Habitual offender: 26 or more years old

On the basis of classification, physical condition, and other factors learned during intake, the inmate is assigned to a specific prison unit.

WORK All inmates must do some type of work unless there is some reason they cannot. Approximately three quarters have active work assignments, primarily in unit support, agriculture, and industry. The rest have medical problems, are in transit, are locked up for severe discipline problems, or for some other reason cannot work. Most work assignments fall into one of these categories:

- Unit support—food and laundry services
- Agriculture—farming to raise food and textiles
- Industry—manufacture of prison uniforms, cleaning supplies, license plates, furniture, and highway signs; renovation of school buses for local school districts

PRISON ROUTINE Prison life is highly regulated. Inmates must wear uniforms. They must shower and change uniforms daily. They must adhere to strict grooming codes, including short hair and being clean shaven for male inmates and no extreme haircuts for female inmates.

Personal property is also limited. Inmates may not possess unapproved clothing. They may possess only limited personal property. Contraband includes money, dice, and playing cards. In short, inmates can have only items issued or specifically authorized by the Institutional Division.

Visitation and correspondence are also limited. Inmates may mail sealed correspondence only to court or government officials. All other mail is read and censored by prison employees. Mail with threats or secret codes is not sent out.

Visitation is allowed only on weekends. Visitors must be on a list of visitors preapproved by prison officials. Each inmate is limited to one 2-hour visit with no more than two adults.

Perhaps the best way to describe prison life is to follow one inmate on a typical day. What follows is a fictional story based upon my own observations and interviews on a recent trip to one of our newer prison units.

An Inmate's Day "Home" was a 9 × 12 concrete and metal cell. It was furnished with two metal slabs protruding from the outside wall to form "bunk beds"; a metal slab protruding from the next wall, with a long narrow slab above it and a fixed metal stool, to form a "desk"; and a metal paneled wall containing a small stainless steel sink, an open commode, and a small piece of reflective material that served as a mirror. Next to the commode was a solid metal door with a small opening; the final wall was bare. Light came from a single fixture built into the sink area and two 1 × 4 grated windows running parallel to the bunks. A small knob next to each window allowed the screened window to be partially opened. The floor and ceiling were concrete. There was no air conditioning; a "forced air" system provided some circulation. Small fans, bought at the inmate's expense, are allowed. "Home," one of 24 such cells in the cell block, which shares five showers and a dayroom, housed two inmates. The dayroom consisted of stainless steel tables, fixed metal stools, some benches, and a color TV with a 30-channel cable, mounted 10 feet off the floor.

Inmate John Smith (a fictional composite) was serving a 20-year sentence for burglary in Dallas County. His "rap" sheet included three misdemeanor arrests. His first felony, burglary of a storage shed, resulted in probation. The probation was revoked when he was convicted of a new felony, burglary of a habitation (the police had agreed to file only one charge after he had helped them recover property from the other seven burglaries he had committed). He received two 5-year sentences—one on the probation revocation and one on the new burglary—which ran concurrently. He served 5 months in the Dallas County jail before he was paroled directly from jail without going to prison. He received his 20-year sentence after he was caught coming out of a house after committing still another burglary. Only Smith and his fences know how many burglaries he had actually done in his career. After being processed at the diagnostic unit near Huntsville, he was sent on a prison bus to his "home" at one of the newer prison units located in Central Texas, where some 2,900 inmates were housed. What follows is a day in inmate Smith's life—one of 730 such days he would serve before his first chance for parole.

5:00 A.M. The intercom announces wake-up for first-shift inmates. Smith has one hour before he reports to work. He waits for his cell mate to use the toilet, then rises. He uses the toilet, brushes his teeth, and shaves. His cell door, which was locked all night, is now unlocked from the outside. He heads from his cell block to the cafeteria building, where breakfast is being served. He has 20 minutes to eat after he arrives. Breakfast today consists of scrambled eggs, grits, biscuits with white gravy, and a choice of milk or coffee. Utensils are plastic forks and spoons (no knives); dishes are a plastic cup and plate. The cafeteria consists of numerous stainless steel tables, each with four fixed stools. Service is cafeteria style: entrees are served by inmates who work in the cafeteria; other items are self-service.

After breakfast, Smith strolls back to his cell block. He still has time to obtain a change of clothes from the laundry cart and to take a shower in one of the five showers in his cell block. Now fed, showered, and in a clean white cotton uniform (a change of clothes is provided each day), he leaves his cell block and makes the short walk to his work assignment at the garment factory.

6:00 A.M. Work begins at the garment factory. The factory is a large, air-conditioned room where up to 200 inmates work at each shift. It is thoroughly modern—clean, neat, spacious—with a minimum of noise. The factory makes uniforms, socks, and winter coats. Most of the work is automated. Smith takes his place behind his assigned knitting machine. He and one second-shift inmate are the only two who use this machine. He makes sure the thread is loaded properly, turns the machine on, and watches as it turns out sock after sock. He monitors the machine and restocks it with thread as needed. He takes one coffee break at mid-morning. During his six-hour shift, his machine will produce hundreds of socks.

12:00 P.M. Smith's shift ends. He walks back toward the cafeteria. It is now daylight and he sees the wide expanses of grass between each building. The grass areas have numerous flower beds, some shaped like the state of Texas. Along the walls of the building, roses have been planted.

12:10 P.M. After a short walk, Smith enters the cafeteria. Lunch is the biggest meal of the day. Smith is served spaghetti with meat sauce and helps himself to pinto beans, peas, carrots, cornbread, and iced tea. Dessert is chocolate cake.

12:30 P.M. Smith heads to the medical building. Since he has been in prison one year, he is entitled to a dental check-up and cleaning. After he is allowed entrance by a guard who checks to make sure he has an appointment, he enters the lobby area. On his right is an 11,000-volume general library; on his left is a functional, well-stocked law library. He proceeds to the medical area, straight ahead. Once inside, he sees the modern, well-lit medical hall, where the signs indicate ophthalmology, podiatry, pharmacy, X-ray, laboratory, and emergency. He turns left and enters the dental department. Three dentists serve the inmate population, and he is seen quickly and given his check-up and teeth cleaning. Smith's teeth are fine, but one other inmate is having a tooth filled and a second is being fitted for dentures.

1:15 P.M. When Smith is done with his dental appointment, he stops by the library on his way out. The library is spacious, well-lit, and staffed by three inmates and one correctional officer. Smith stops by the periodicals and checks out the headlines of the *Dallas Morning News,* his hometown paper. He then proceeds to the mystery section to see if Sue Grafton's alphabet mystery books have been updated. He is disappointed to find that *G Is for Gumshoe* (published in 1990) is still the latest book available. He then leaves the library and returns to his cell block area.

1:30 P.M. Smith has the remainder of the day free. He has several options. In the exercise yard, he can play volleyball, basketball, or use the weight machines. The same activities are offered in the gym. In the dayroom, he can watch cable color TV, or play chess or dominoes. The "piddling room" is a craft shop where he can do leather making, woodworking, or drawing. In the commissary, Smith can buy snacks, food, hygiene items, shaving supplies, art supplies, paper, and small electronic items, if he has the money. (He has no wages, but relatives can send money or he can sell craft items.) Some sample items, with costs (tax included), are

Dr. Pepper (12 oz.): $.40

Blue Bell Ice Cream (pint): $1.30

Milky Way: $.45

Vienna sausage: $.60

Hershey's Syrup: $.55

Moon Pie: $.30

Colgate toothpaste: $1.05

Irish Spring soap: $.15

Tums: $.55

Box fan (10″): $11.50

Memory typewriter: $200.00

Sunglasses: $3.65

5:30 P.M. Smith walks over to the cafeteria for dinner. The same cafeteria-style routine is followed. The menu is chicken gumbo rice, black-eyed peas, corn, carrots, greens, and biscuits. The beverage is water.

6:00 P.M. Smith has the remainder of the evening for free time. If he chooses, he can spend three hours of his evening in college class. Regular school is free. College classes require tuition comparable to hourly rates charged at state colleges. Vocational education is also an option. Academic classes are taught in fully equipped classrooms with one teacher and one aide for classes of 22–28 students. The rooms have books, reference materials, maps, and bulletin boards; they are virtually indistinguishable from public school classrooms. Since Smith is not enrolled in school this semester, he has the same free-time options he had in the afternoon.

10:30 P.M. Rack up. The dayroom is closed; Smith and his cell mate must be in their cell. The door is locked from the outside.

PROGRAMS

Education Educational programs range from basic literacy to college level. The Wyndham School District operates exclusively for inmates. All new inmates are tested for basic literacy. Those who test below a sixth-grade reading level must attend reading classes. Those who attain that reading level may enroll in secondary courses in both academic and vocational areas. They may get a high school degree. The Wyndham School District offers courses that roughly parallel those in the public school system. The district also provides bilingual, remedial, and special education classes.

Substance Abuse Treatment Each unit in the Institutional Division has a substance abuse counselor. These counselors arrange individual or group counseling for any inmate with a drug or alcohol problem. These programs are voluntary, although some inmates must attend.

Sex Offender Treatment The Sexual Offender Treatment Program is a 24-month therapy program. It is available only for inmates who volunteer and who are nearing the end of their sentences.

Chaplaincy Program Each Institutional Division unit has a chapel and a chaplain. The chaplain is available to provide spiritual support to inmates. Religious services are regularly conducted for various faiths.

Legal Programs The Staff Counsels for Offenders is a group of lawyers employed by the Texas Department of Criminal Justice to help inmates with legal problems such as jail-time credits, termination of parental rights, or post-conviction writs of habeas corpus. Each unit also maintains a law library which the inmates may use.

FURLOUGH Until 1995, Texas had one of the most liberal furlough programs in the nation. For example, so-called Appropriate Reason Furloughs were allowed for up to 10 days for any reason that would help reform an inmate. Inmates were released on an honor system to visit family members or conduct business.

That furlough program was abolished and replaced with a very limited emergency-absence program. This new program requires that the inmate be escorted by a guard. Emergency absences are available only for medical or psychiatric diagnosis or treatment, for funerals, or for visiting critically ill relatives.

RELEASE Inmates released from prison get a set of civilian clothes and $100. If released on parole, the inmates get half of the money on release and the remaining half when they report to the parole officer.

PAROLE Parole is early release from prison—that is, before inmates have completed their entire sentences. They will serve the rest of the sentence on parole. Inmates become eligible after serving a percentage of their sentences, which is set by the legislature. Eligible inmates must then be approved by the parole board. Approved inmates are released as long as they obey conditions similar to probation conditions. If they violate a condition, they can be returned to custody and have their parole revoked.

The responsibility for parole is divided between two groups: the Board of Pardons and Paroles (parole board) and the Pardons and Paroles Division of the Texas Department of Criminal Justice (Paroles Division). The parole board has 18 full-time members appointed by the governor. The parole board makes discretionary decisions to grant, deny, or revoke a parole. The Paroles Division supervises the parolee in a manner similar to that of probation officers.

102,256 convicted felons are on parole in Texas.

Source: Texas Department of Criminal Justice

PAROLE ELIGIBILITY All inmates are eligible for parole after serving some percentage of their sentences. Inmates sentenced to death or those convicted of state jail felonies or misdemeanors are not eligible for parole. Parole eligibility depends on two factors: the type of offense committed and the date it was committed. Generally, inmates convicted of violent crimes must serve a larger percentage of their sentence than those convicted of nonviolent crimes. The legislature has specifically designated violent crimes as

- murder
- capital murder
- aggravated kidnapping
- aggravated robbery
- aggravated sexual assault
- indecency with a child by contact
- sexual assault of a child
- sexual assault of an adult
- any felony where the judgment shows that the inmate used or exhibited a deadly weapon

A deadly weapon can be a firearm or anything else that, as it was used or intended to be used, could cause death or serious bodily injury. Deadly weapons can include nearly any physical object, such as scissors, string, or a baseball bat. They can also include a vehicle driven by an intoxicated driver.

Inmates convicted of any of these violent offenses are often referred to as "3g offenders." This name comes from the section of the Code of Criminal Procedure (Article 42.12, Section 3g) that lists these crimes. Those 3g offenders who committed their crimes after August 31, 1993, must serve the lesser of half the sentence or 30 calendar years. The sentence must be served in calendar time; no good-time credits are allowed for 3g offenders. The 3g offender must serve a minimum of 2 calendar years regardless of the actual sentence.

Because of the 30-calendar-year maximum, 60 years is the longest effective sentence a criminal can get. In other words, half of the 60-year sentence is 30 calendar years—the maximum a criminal can serve before being eligible for parole. Sentences of 61 to 99 years or life are, for parole purposes, identical to 60 years.

Inmates who committed 3g crimes before September 1, 1993, are subject to shorter times-served before parole eligibility dates. If the offense was committed between September 1, 1987, and August 31, 1993, the inmate must serve the lesser of a quarter of his sentence or 15 calendar years. The 2-year minimum also applies. Again, for parole purposes, 60 years is the maximum possible sentence. Inmates who committed 3g crimes between September 1, 1977, and August 31, 1987, have to serve the lesser of one third of their sentence or 20 calendar years. The 2-year minimum and the effective 60-year maximum apply. Before September 1, 1977, there was no 3g classification and all inmates became eligible for parole after serving the same percentage of their sentences.

Non-3g offenders who committed their crime after August 31, 1987, must serve the lesser of one quarter of their sentence or 15 years. This is not calendar time. Good-time credits can greatly reduce the actual amount of time served. As with 3g offenders, the 15-year maximum makes 60 years the longest effective sentence for parole purposes. Non-3g offenders with sentences of 61 to 99 years or life are eligible for parole when they have credit for 15 years.

Good-time credit is awarded by the Institutional Division. It is given to inmates who maintain good conduct and diligently participate in work and education programs. Generally, inmates may receive 45 additional days' credit for every 30 days actually served. Thus, they receive a total of 75 days' credit toward parole eligibility for each 30 days served. The rules regarding good time are fairly complex. However, the general figure of 75 days of credit for 30 days of actual service is a basic figure which can be used to estimate parole eligibility for non-3g offenders.

The effect of good time can best be shown by an example. John Smith receives a 10-year sentence. He must have credit for a quarter of the sentence to be eligible for parole. He receives two and a half months of credit (75 days) for each month (30 days) he actually serves. Thus, John can become eligible for parole after serving only one year.

> 12 months served × 2.5 months good time = 30 months' credit (¼ of the original 10 years)

Rather than doing these calculations each time, just divide any sentence by 10. This gives a rough estimate of the actual calendar time that inmates with good behavior must serve before becoming eligible for parole. Remember, too, that they will serve the rest of their sentence under parole supervision.

Also remember that the maximum sentence for parole purposes is 60 years. Divided by 10, that's 6 calendar years for non-3g offenders. Inmates with bad behavior may have to serve considerably more time on their sentences.

PAROLE ELIGIBILITY MADE EASY

The discussion of parole eligibility may make your eyes glaze over. If so, remember that it can be reduced to three simple rules. These rules apply only to current crimes and not to people who were convicted of crimes committed before September 1, 1993.

Rule 1: Violent Offenders
Violent offenses are aggravated sexual assault, aggravated robbery, aggravated kidnapping, murder, indecency with a child (by contact), sexual assault, or any crime where a deadly weapon is used. Minimum time served before eligible for parole consideration is the lesser of one half of the sentence or 30 calendar years.

Rule 2: Capital Murder
When the death penalty is not given, minimum time served before eligible for parole consideration is 40 calendar years.

Rule 3: All Other Felonies
Minimum time served before eligible for parole consideration is the lesser of 1⁄10 of the sentence or 6 calendar years.

CONSECUTIVE SENTENCES When defendants are convicted of two or more crimes, the sentences automatically run concurrently (together) unless the judge orders them stacked, or run consecutively (one after the other). If the judge orders the sentences stacked, the inmates must become eligible for parole on the first sentence before they begin to serve the second sentence. Also, they must be eligible for parole on all of the sentences before they can be considered for actual release on parole.

Consecutive sentences can dramatically increase the actual time served by an inmate. For example, if inmate John Smith receives two consecutive life sentences for 3g offenses which occurred after August 31, 1993, he must serve 60 calendar years before he can first be considered for parole.

BEGIN DATE A sentence's begin date includes all time served in custody on the current conviction. Thus, if John Smith spends one year in jail before his conviction, the judge must begin his sentence on the day he begins his confinement. Inmates are not entitled to credit for time spent while they are free on bond.

CAPITAL MURDER Up until 1991, inmates convicted of capital murder and serving life sentences were treated the same as other 3g offenders. As of September 1, 1991, capital murder inmates with a life sentence had to serve 35 calendar years to become eligible for parole. Another law, effective September 1, 1993, increased this to 40 calendar years. As with all forms of parole eligibility, the laws in effect on the date the crime was committed control parole eligibility.

DRUG-FREE ZONES Texas makes one other exception to the general parole eligibility rules. A drug-free zone is an area on or within 1,000 feet of a school or playground *or* on or within 300 feet of a youth center, public pool, or video arcade. Inmates convicted of delivery offenses in these zones must serve the lesser of five calendar years or their actual sentence in calendar years.

MANDATORY SUPERVISION Mandatory supervision is a type of parole where the release is automatic. Inmates must be released on mandatory supervision when the actual calendar time served plus all good-time credits equals the total sentence.

In response to public criticism about the "automatic" nature of mandatory supervision, the legislature created a fail-safe mechanism for dangerous inmates. This allows the parole board to deny release to an otherwise qualified inmate if the board finds that, despite good conduct time, the inmate's release would endanger the public.

Mandatory supervision began in 1977 and applied to all felons. Certain crimes committed after August 31, 1987, were excluded from the list of offenses eligible for mandatory supervision. The list has been modified several times. Inmates with convictions (either their present or a previous offense) are currently excluded from mandatory supervision eligibility:

- capital murder
- first- or second-degree murder
- first- or second-degree aggravated kidnapping
- indecency with a child
- aggravated sexual assault or sexual assault

- aggravated robbery or robbery
- first-degree injury to a child, elderly individual, or disabled individual
- first-degree arson
- first-degree burglary
- first- or second-degree aggravated assault
- any felony with a deadly weapon finding
- delivery of drugs in a drug-free zone
- delivery of drugs where the defendant involved a child under 18 in the offense

When inmates are released on mandatory supervision, they are subject to the same conditions as a parolee. Mandatory supervision can be revoked just as parole can, and the inmate can be returned to prison.

PAROLE APPROVAL PROCESS The parole process begins shortly after an inmate arrives at the Institutional Division. Information is gathered and an estimated parole date is established.

Months before the parole date, a computer generates a list of potential parolees for the Transitional Planning Department. A case manager interviews the inmate and develops a parole plan. This plan includes residence and employment plans. In Austin, the Paroles Division prepares the inmate's file for a parole board member.

At the same time, the Paroles Division notifies the trial officials so that they can make written comments about the proposed parole. The trial officials are the sentencing judge, the district attorney, and the sheriff. If a change of venue was granted, the trial officials in both the county of conviction and the county where the crime occurred are notified. Also, the Paroles Division notifies victims who have so requested.

The chair of the parole board assigns the case to a three-member parole panel. One member of the panel will review the file and conduct an in-person interview with the inmate. That member will vote and forward the file to the other two members, who will also vote. Two of the three votes are required to take action. The parole panel has three options:

- approve the inmate's release to parole
- deny parole and set a continued review date to consider the parole again in one to three years
- deny parole and order a serve-all, meaning the inmate will remain in prison until mandatory supervision or discharge

If the panel approves a parole, the information in the parole plan goes to a field office to be verified or investigated. If the parole plan is approved, the parole receives its final approval and victims who have so requested are informed of the release date.

Finally, prison officials prepare the inmate for release. The inmate is released with instructions to report to a parole officer by a certain time.

PRE-PAROLE TRANSFER Not all inmates are paroled directly from prison. Non-3g inmates may be transferred to a pre-parole transfer (PPT) facility six months before their anticipated parole. PPTs are minimum-security facilities where special vocational and transitional services are available. While at a PPT, inmates are assigned to a parole officer who will make written reports on their progress. If the inmates fail to maintain proper behavior, they can be transferred back to prison and have their parole canceled.

PAROLE IN ABSENTIA During the late 1980s and early 1990s, tens of thousands of inmates were paroled and released without actually going to a prison. These were inmates with short non-3g convictions who become eligible for parole while waiting in county jail to be transferred to the Institutional Division. Although the legal authority for parole in absentia still exists, it has become practically nonexistent since the mid-1990s because of the completion of the massive prison construction program which—temporarily at least—has eliminated the prison overcrowding.

56,376 convicted felons who received prison sentences were paroled directly from county jails without doing a day in prison during the years 1988–1995.

Source: Texas Department of Criminal Justice, Paroles Division

PAROLE SUPERVISION Parole supervision is similar to probation supervision. The Paroles Division employs parole officers who monitor and supervise parolees. The conditions of parole release, set by the parole board, can include any condition imposed on a probationer. In addition to those conditions, the parole board can impose any of the following:

- no communication with or presence near the residence or normal places frequented by the victim in a stalking case
- an $8 monthly fee to the Crime Victims' Compensation Fund

- if convicted of a sexual offense, a $5 monthly fee to the sexual assault fund

Supervision of inmates released on mandatory supervision is identical to supervision of other parolees. Parole supervision has three levels of intensity.

Minimum Parolees on minimum supervision must report in person once a month to a parole officer. The parole officer must make home visits at least twice during the first six months and must verify employment.

Medium Parolees on medium supervision must report in person once a month to a parole officer. At least every other month, the parole officer must make home visits and verify employment and residence. The officer may also contact the parolees' relatives, friends, and employers as needed.

Intensive Parolees on intensive supervision must report to a parole officer at least 10 times per month. At least once a week, they must report in person.

Annual Reporting Status Parolees who complete one year of supervision without violation can be given annual reporting status. These parolees are not actively supervised and must mail in a written report once a year. Rules now in the approval process would require inmates to serve more than one year of supervision before being eligible for annual reporting status.

No-Report Status In no-report status, parolees are on parole but they do not have to report in. To be eligible for no-report status, parolees must have served at least half of the release period and must have made a good faith effort to comply with any restitution orders. The Paroles Division must determine whether this status is in the best interest of society.

PAROLE REVOCATION Parolees who violate the conditions of parole may be arrested and have their parole conditions modified or the parole revoked. Such parolees are entitled to a hearing before the parole board's designee or a panel of the parole board.

10,666 parolees had their paroles revoked in 2002.

Source: Texas Department of Criminal Justice Annual Report

If the parolee is convicted of a new felony offense, this conviction can substitute for the parole board hearing. However, the parolee, by then an inmate again, may still request a hearing, which is limited to mitigating evidence.

STATE AND COUNTY JAIL OFFENSES So far, this chapter has covered punishments for capital and first-, second-, and third-degree felonies. Punishments for state jail felonies and misdemeanors are different.

STATE JAIL FELONIES The state jail provides for shorter but more certain sentences than the prison system. State jail felonies are the lowest levels of felony crimes. Many inmates who are now being punished in the state jail system are the ones who previously avoided prison by receiving parole in absentia from the county jail. Several characteristics make punishments for state jail felonies (SJFs) different from punishments for other felonies:

- Sentences are served in calendar time; there is no good time.
- There is no parole.
- For many first-time drug possession offenders, probation is automatic.
- The judge may order confinement for up to 1 year if the SJF is drug delivery or for up to 6 months for other crimes.
- The judge may order the inmate released on probation at any time after he or she has served at least 75 days in the state jail.

With these exceptions, the SJF is treated the same as other felonies. The judges can defer adjudication and impose identical conditions of probation. The same rules for revocation apply to both SJFs and regular felonies.

MISDEMEANORS Misdemeanor punishments are similar to those for felonies with two exceptions: the place of confinement is a county jail rather than a prison, and there is no parole.

The chief early release mechanism from county jail is good time. Inmates can earn good-time credits for good behavior and work. The local sheriff sets these policies. An inmate may not have his or her sentence reduced by more than two-thirds by good time.

The first four chapters have dealt with the system and how it functions. The crime and then the criminal are the main focus of the system. Now it is time to turn to the crime victim. The next chapter details the rights which a crime victim has.

CHAPTER 5

VICTIMS' RIGHTS

Victim.

It is such an anonymous word. It is a word that can obscure pain, a word that, combined with a maze of statistics and theories, lets us forget the very human side of crime. Like most criminal justice professionals, I became a prosecutor out of a general sense of wanting to do something about crime—to put the bad guys behind bars. During my early career, I handled routine drug and burglary cases. The focus really was on the bad guys. But as my career progressed to handling more violent crimes—rapes, robberies, murders, child molesting—I dealt more and more with victims.

To me, "victim" was no longer an abstract concept. Gradually, victims became faces, faces of people hurting. And not just the individual person hurt by a crime, but the husband, wife, mother, father, grandparent, and child—all of the people whose lives are changed by a single violent crime.

A victim became the young woman who was raped and beaten so badly that her face was unrecognizable and her unborn child was killed by the trauma. Or the two little boys who will never be able to run because a drunk driver rammed their mother's car head on. Or the young mother who holds her infant daughter as her husband is gunned down in front of her and her family.

These victims do not ask to be part of any system. They do not want to be crippled or robbed. They do not want one of their loved ones to be murdered. They become part of the system because a criminal forces them to become part of the system. When they do, they learn quickly. The system is designed primarily to protect the rights of the criminals who thrust them into the system to begin with.

It is the criminals who must be given the Miranda warnings. It is the criminals who must receive free lawyers if they cannot afford one. It is the criminals whose rights to privacy must be scrupulously protected as the police investigate the crime. It is the criminals whose every legal right must be carefully protected at trial. It is the criminals whose family and friends will ask judges for mercy when they are finally convicted. It is the criminals who will be given free education, medical care, room and board, and drug treatment when they are finally in prison.

No one would argue that we should not have procedures in place to ensure that trials are fair. No one wants to convict innocent people. But it should be equally obvious that victims also deserve fair treatment. And, although the system's treatment of victims can still improve, much progress has been made. Consider, for example, that in the last 20 years Texas has

- developed a Crime Victims' Compensation program that annually reimburses violent crime victims more than $70 million for such things as uninsured medical expenses and lost wages
- mandated that judges order defendants to pay restitution to their victims
- provided an avenue for formal input from victims both by a written victim impact statement and by an opportunity for victims to address the court after sentencing
- mandated that every prosecutor's office and law enforcement agency have a victims' assistance coordinator on their staff
- provided victims with notification of parole and an opportunity to protest parole release decisions
- developed a network of rape crisis programs and battered women's shelters around the state

These and the many other laws detailed in this chapter are a good beginning. But these procedures need to be expanded, refined, and improved. Victims deserve a system that treats them with respect and dignity.

BACKGROUND Barely 25 years ago, if you were a crime victim, you had no rights. The criminal justice system treated you, at best, with indifference and, at worst, with open hostility. Certainly, some law enforcement officers, prosecutors, and judges treated you with respect and gave you information. But they acted in spite of a system best described as antivictim.

Consider this: twenty-five years ago Mary Jones, a rape victim, would very likely have reported the crime to a hostile male police officer. He would have taken Mary to a hospital emergency room for a rape exam. Privacy and respect would have varied from hospital to hospital. Mary would have had to pay for the exam. She would then have had to convince the police that she had in fact been raped. Mary might have had to pass a polygraph examination before they would have taken her "claim" seriously.

Mary Jones could expect hostility or indifference throughout the system. If her rapist was arrested, she likely would not have known what was happening as the case progressed. If the case went to trial, Mary—not her rapist—would have been the focus of the trial. To discredit her testimony, the defense lawyer would have asked about Mary's past sexual experiences. Her clothing and behavior would have been extensively cross-examined.

Mary would have faced this hostility with no formal assistance: no victim advocates, no rape crisis centers, no free counseling, no help from anywhere in the system.

Rape victims weren't the only mistreated victims. Child molesters were seldom prosecuted. DWIs routinely pled guilty to lesser charges. When the DWI caused death or bodily injury, a probated sentence would likely have been the most that would have followed.

Judges seldom ordered restitution to any victims. The police kept stolen property as evidence and did not return it to victims. Victims could not expect information about the progress of the case, the court setting, or the plea negotiations. There were no victim compensation programs. The prosecutors and judges treated victims as necessary burdens. If victims were witnesses, they were told when to show up in court. That was about it.

In the mid-1970s, all of this began to change. First, rape victims banded together to insist on better treatment. Rape crisis centers were started to support them. Volunteers went with them to police stations, hospitals, and courthouses. The volunteers gave support and information, and they advocated for humane treatment. As the media began to draw attention to rape victims, legislatures passed tougher rape laws. New shield laws excluded testimony on a rape victim's prior sexual experiences. Law enforcement officers, judges, and prosecutors became more aware of the needs of rape victims. Juries became less hostile toward them.

Drunk driving victims were the next to band together. Starting in the early 1980s, their progress followed that of rape victims. Mothers Against Drunk Driving forced the media to pay attention. The media helped to change the public's attitude. Suddenly, drunk driving was no longer socially acceptable. Tougher laws were passed. Law enforcement officers, judges, and prosecutors changed their attitudes. Ultimately, juries became much less tolerant of drunk drivers.

Child molestation victims next followed the pattern. What began as a few outspoken child advocates led to a significantly heightened media awareness by 1984. The media attention increased public awareness, which led to vastly increased reporting of child molesting. Tougher laws made the system less hostile to children. Law enforcement officers, judges, and prosecutors responded. Finally, juries were willing to believe a child's testimony.

Also during the 1980s, groups started advocating general reforms in the criminal justice system. Some groups were started by victims or survivors of individual crimes. Other groups rose in a community shocked by an individual crime. Collectively, these victim advocates were able to initiate reforms that forced the system to recognize and respond to the voice of the victim. The Crime Victim Bill of Rights is now part of the Texas constitution. A host of laws either implement the Bill of Rights or address a specific problem.

CRIME VICTIM LAWS Over the past twenty-five years, the Texas Legislature has passed laws to protect the rights of crime victims. Because of the time period over which they were enacted, and because of the number of changes, they were scattered throughout the various Texas criminal laws.

Symbolically, the most important such law is the Crime Victim Bill of Rights in the Texas constitution. These rights are set out at the end of a list of rights guaranteed to criminal defendants. The Texas constitution guarantees crime victims

- the right to fair treatment and to respect for their dignity and privacy
- the right to reasonable protection from the defendant

The constitution also guarantees five additional rights if the victim requests them:

- the right to be notified of court proceedings
- the right to be present at all public court proceedings (unless the judge determines that the victim is going to testify and that testimony would be materially affected by the victim's presence while others testify)
- the right to confer with the prosecutor

- the right to restitution
- the right to information about the conviction, sentence, imprisonment, and release of the offender

Although these constitutional protections are largely symbolic, the legislature has enacted specific legislation to implement them. The legislature has also passed a Crime Victims' Rights Law; it lists many of these rights and funds the means to ensure them. The Crime Victims' Rights Law is designed specifically for victims of violent crimes. It defines victims as people who are "the victim of sexual assault, kidnapping, aggravated robbery," or people who have "suffered bodily injury or death as a result of the criminal conduct of another." This definition also includes guardians of child victims or incompetent victims and close relatives of deceased victims. Although these rights are mandated for violent crime victims, most of the services and procedures are routinely available to victims of nonviolent crimes as well, with the exception of the right to receive victim compensation payment. The Crime Victims' Rights Law grants victims the right

- to receive from law enforcement agencies protection from harm and threats
- to have the judge consider their safety and their families' safety in setting bail
- to provide information about
  - investigative procedures
  - the defendant's right to bail
  - the criminal justice system in general (e.g., plea negotiations, restitution, appeals, and paroles)
  - prior notification of scheduling or rescheduling of court dates
  - the Crime Victims' Compensation Act
  - parole procedures in general and the status of the defendant in the victim's case, including his or her actual release date
- to provide information about the impact of the crime in the pre-sentence report
- to provide parole board members information prior to their considering parole
- to a separate and secure waiting room during court proceedings
- to prompt return of property held by a law enforcement agency when it is no longer needed as evidence
- to have the prosecutor notify the victim's employer that the employee must be absent from work to attend court proceedings

- to receive counseling about HIV and AIDS in the case of sexual assault
- to be present, subject to the approval of the judge, at all public court proceedings
- to have law enforcement agencies pay for medical examinations used to investigate sexual assault cases

Also under the Crime Victims' Rights Law, law enforcement agencies and prosecutors' offices designate individuals to ensure these rights. A nearly identical list of victims' rights is provided in the Family Code when the defendant is a juvenile. The juvenile law also provides for the local juvenile board to ensure that victims are granted these rights.

NELL MYERS: A TRIBUTE

When Nina Nell Myers, the godmother of Texas crime victims' rights, died on September 26, 2000, Texas lost its most well-known advocate for the rights of crime victims.

Nell was one of the first champions for giving victims a real voice in the criminal justice system. It was not a role for which she volunteered. Nell was thrust into it by a personal tragedy. Her daughter Cydney was murdered in 1979.

At first no one paid any attention to Nell. She was, after all, just another grieving mother. The system was designed to protect the rights of the accused. Victims had no rights and no voice. But Nell didn't take "no" for an answer. She founded the group People Against Violent Crime, mobilized other victims, and lobbied the legislature. By 1985, her efforts had amended the Texas Constitution by adding a Victim Bill of Rights. From then on there was a string of legislative and policy victories that assured victims a meaningful role in the system.

Why was Nell successful? Her cause was just and the facts of her story and those of many other victims were compelling. And then there were Nell's methods, which led to her being called "feisty" and "a bulldog." Perhaps Verna Lee Carr, her friend and coworker from People Against Violent Crime, described her best when she said, "She was a hell-raiser, a little old hell-raiser."

But in reality, Nell was just a mother. A mother who saw an unjust system and changed it. I'm just glad I could call her my friend.

SPECIFIC CRIME VICTIMS' LAWS In addition to the constitution and the Crime Victims' Rights Law, other laws protect crime victims. This section discusses such laws in the order in which they affect a victim.

INFORMATION FROM LAW ENFORCEMENT AGENCY A law enforcement agency must give the victim of a violent crime certain written information. This information is usually provided in a brochure or similar form and includes information about

- available emergency and medical services
- rights to compensation under the Crime Victims' Compensation Act and to payment for a medical exam for sexual assault victims
- social service agency programs
- procedures to contact victim coordinators at the law enforcement agency and prosecutor's office
- investigative procedures
- defendant's right to bail
- rights of victims detailed in the Crime Victims' Rights Law

PROTECTION BY POLICE Victims are entitled to receive from law enforcement agencies adequate protection from harm and threats that arise from their efforts to assist the prosecution. Obviously, law enforcement agencies can only do their best. However, they get help from laws on bail, from protective orders, and from special laws that allow family violence defendants to be held in jail even after they have posted bond.

SETTING OF BAIL AMOUNT AND CONDITIONS The victim has the right for the judge to consider victims and their families' safety when setting bond. The judge can also consider the community's safety. The judge may apply special conditions to a bond for stalkers or sexual offenders whose victims are 12 or younger. These conditions may prohibit the offender from directly communicating with the victim and from going near the school, residence, or other places frequented by the victim. For child sexual assault offenders, these bond conditions can, for up to 90 days, override a court order granting possession of or visitation with the child.

VICTIM NOTIFICATION Victims are entitled to a number of different types of information and notifications. Some of these notifications include:

• release of the defendant on bond (domestic violence and stalking cases only)

• change in probation status (placing of the offender on probation, any change in the conditions of probation, or a hearing to revoke or end probation)

• release of the defendant/offender by a jail, prison, or other such facility (domestic violence cases only)

• the offender's escape from or death in a state prison facility

185,299 acts of family violence were reported to law enforcement agencies in 2003.

Source: DPS, Texas Department of Public Safety, Crime in Texas, 2003

FAMILY VIOLENCE PREVENTION The law defines *family* broadly to include former spouses and all people living together in the same dwelling. *Family violence* means the intentional use or threat of force by a family member against another family member. Such force does not include reasonable discipline of a child.

To help prevent family violence, law enforcement officers must now follow certain procedures when they respond to a family violence call. They must give written notice in both Spanish and English that physical assault is a crime even if committed by a household member. The written notice must spell out the victim's right to file charges with the local prosecutor and to apply for a protective order. Finally, the notice must include the phone number of the local family violence shelter or other similar services for family violence victims.

The officer must also write a report detailing the incident. This report must be available to other police officers and the prosecutor. In addition, the law enforcement agency must provide its officers with access to and details about protective orders.

A NEEDED REFUGE

It happened again. He promised the last time that he would never hit her again. After all, she was pregnant with their second child. But tonight his rage was worse than ever before and Marsha was all but certain what the pain in her rib cage meant. He had broken a bone this time.

As she dialed the hotline number, she couldn't help but wonder how this could happen to her. She was smart and attractive. She had a great job, a nice home, a bright two-year-old son. Surely this happened to other women, not her.

Marsha was able to gather her son and a few belongings and sneak out of the house to the local battered women's shelter. There Marsha found a few days of calm—valuable time to begin picking up the pieces of her life.

Although Marsha is a fictional composite, her story happens throughout Texas with alarming frequency. Approximately 29,000 women and children escape batterers by going to shelters each year.

The first shelter in Texas was opened in 1977 in Austin. Since then, a network of 76 shelters has been developed across the state. The Texas Council on Family Violence, headquartered in Austin, provides training for and technical assistance to the shelters.

In addition to providing a safe place to stay for women and children, shelters provide hotlines, emergency medical care, counseling, employment services, and a host of information and referral services. Shelter groups also provide public education and follow-up services for former residents or battered women who have never been residents.

PROTECTIVE ORDERS In a protective order, a court directs an individual to do something or to stop doing something. Protective orders are available to prevent family violence. A private lawyer or a prosecutor can get a protective order. If a prosecutor gets it, the victim pays no lawyer fees.

A judge can issue a protective order after finding that family violence has occurred and is likely to occur again soon. A judge has broad authority to order necessary actions in a protective order. These orders may require a family member for up to one year to

- attend counseling
- complete a batterers' treatment program
- vacate the residence
- not communicate with other family members
- not go near the residence, business, school, or child care facility where another family member may be present
- stop committing family violence
- stop threatening other family members

Violation of a protective order is a crime punishable as a Class A misdemeanor. If the family member violates the protective order by committing a separate crime, he or she may be prosecuted for both the violation of the protective order and the separate crime.

Emergency protective orders may be issued by judges, who give defendants their legal warnings after arrest. These emergency protective orders are available only for family violence and stalking cases. The orders must be in writing and a copy of an order must be given to defendants while they are in court. Judges may issue such orders even if no one requests one. These emergency orders are good for 31 days.

SEXUAL ASSAULT MEDICAL EXAMINATION Investigation of sexual assault normally includes a medical examination. The doctor will document injuries and gather evidence, for example, semen, pubic hair, and head hair. The law enforcement agency that requests such an examination pays for it. The agency is not required to pay for any medical treatment that the victim receives at the same time. If a victim's medical insurance does not cover this treatment, the victim can apply for reimbursement under the Crime Victims' Compensation Act.

PROHIBITION OF POLYGRAPH EXAMINATION OF SEXUAL ASSAULT VICTIM Even as recently as 1995, a small number of law enforcement agencies required some victims of sexual assaults to first pass a polygraph examination before their complaint would be investigated. This practice was prohibited in 1995; no law enforcement agency may require a victim to submit to a polygraph. Under certain limited circumstances, a prosecutor may request that a victim take such an exam. However, a prosecutor may not dismiss a case solely because a victim did not take or did not pass such an examination.

HIV/AIDS COUNSELING AND TESTING Victims of sexual assault, aggravated sexual assault, and indecency with a child by contact are entitled to counseling and testing information about HIV and AIDS. This requirement is usually met by a referral to a local public health agency or an HIV/AIDS information service.

Victims of these crimes are also entitled to request an HIV/AIDS test of defendants after they are indicted. A second such test can be ordered after defendants are convicted.

INFORMATION FROM PROSECUTOR Prosecutors must give certain information in writing to the victims of violent crime:

- an overview of each stage of the criminal justice process: bail, plea bargaining, parole, restitution, and appeal
- a list of rights under the Crime Victims' Rights Act
- suggested steps for a threatened or intimidated victim

- notification of Crime Victims' Compensation Act benefits
- referral to social service agencies for help
- the case number and the court the case is assigned to
- the victim impact statement
- if requested, notice of court settings, reschedulings, and plea agreements

This information usually comes in a brochure that covers all of the required notifications. Such a brochure is available from the local prosecutor's office. Prosecutors will also provide a blank victim impact statement and the forms to file a crime victim compensation claim.

WAITING ROOM Violent crime victims are also entitled to a separate and secure waiting room. This waiting room gives victims privacy and security during a trial, enabling them to avoid spending long periods of trial time sharing a common waiting area, hallways, and bathrooms with defendants and their relatives. If such a waiting room is not available, other mandatory safeguards, such as allowing victims to wait in the prosecutor's office, minimize the contacts between victims and the defendants and their relatives.

VIDEOTAPED TESTIMONY OF CHILDREN At trial, prosecutors may use as evidence videotapes of children under 13 who are victims of sexual or physical abuse. The same law lets such victims testify by closed-circuit TV or videotape. This law has many technical requirements to protect the rights of defendants. In practice, videotapes seldom substitute for live testimony from a child. For one thing, the circumstances of taping create legal problems. Also, a child testifying as a live witness is more persuasive to a jury than a videotape of the child.

Although a videotape may not eliminate the need for a child victim to testify, it can still be very helpful. For example, taping lets the child tell pretrial investigators what happened just once, instead of many times. After the initial interview, social workers, law enforcement officers, prosecutors, and grand jurors can each view the tape instead of continually reinterviewing the child. It also helps to show the tape to the defense lawyer. Many defendants change their pleas to guilty after their lawyers tell them how believable the child is on the videotape.

CHILD ADVOCACY CENTERS

Susan had not quite turned eight the Friday afternoon she sat quietly sobbing in her second-grade classroom. While the

other children were thinking of the two days of fun and freedom on the weekend, Susan was dreading it. This was her mother's weekend to work the night shift at the local hospital where she was a nurse. And Susan knew that meant her stepfather would be visiting her at night—those awful nights when he would tell her she was pretty, that she was special, and that she had to keep their secret.

Fortunately, Susan's teacher took the time to notice and talk to her. From the time that Susan told, she was never abused again. Her mother supported her and her stepfather was arrested, convicted, and sent to prison.

Also, fortunately, Susan lived in a community served by a children's advocacy center. Rather than being taken to a police station, she was taken to the advocacy center, a small house specifically set aside for child-abuse investigations.

At the center she was interviewed by a specially trained social worker. The interview was videotaped, and the videotape was shared with police and prosecutors and later shown to the grand jurors who indicted Susan's stepfather. Later, when Susan underwent counseling, she went to the same advocacy center to meet with her therapist.

Because of the advocacy center, Susan was able to avoid what is often referred to as revictimization by the system—the process of taking young children to a cold police station where the first of numerous interviews is followed by far too much insensitive treatment and a far too lengthy prosecution.

At the advocacy center a team of social workers, law enforcement personnel, and prosecutors can all work together to coordinate the judicial and social-service response to a case of abuse. The net result is better case screening, better investigations, and more support for the victim.

Texas is a leader in child advocacy centers. One of the first such centers in the nation, The Bridge, opened in Amarillo in 1989. By 2005, Texas had 53 such centers.

PREVIOUS SEXUAL CONDUCT OF SEXUAL ASSAULT VICTIMS Judges do not allow evidence about a sexual assault victim's reputation or about specific instances of the victim's previous sexual behavior. An occasional exception occurs when the victim and the defendant have had a past sexual relationship. A defense lawyer who wants to ask questions about specific sexual acts must first obtain permission from the trial judge.

PRESENCE AT TRIAL A victim has a right to be physically present at any court proceeding. However, at the request of the defense or the prosecution, the judge can exclude any witness, including the victim, while other witnesses testify.

When the victim is also a witness, the judge must decide whether the victim's testimony would be materially affected by hearing the other witnesses testify.

It seems grossly unfair that the defendant can watch the entire trial while the victim cannot. As a practical matter, however, that is exactly what happens. Most trial judges, even those sympathetic to victims' rights, are concerned that allowing the victim into the courtroom could make an appeals court later order a new trial.

The judge can exclude the victim only while other witnesses testify. The victim is always allowed in the courtroom during final arguments. Also, except in very unusual circumstances, the victim is allowed in the courtroom during the punishment phase.

RETURN OF PROPERTY When the prosecutor no longer needs an item for evidence, a victim is entitled to its prompt return. A prosecutor can photograph personal items and return them before a trial. For stolen property, a prosecutor can nearly always use a photograph as evidence in court.

REIMBURSEMENT FOR VICTIM'S TRAVEL Texas has a generous reimbursement policy for witnesses in criminal cases. Any witness who lives outside of Texas or outside of the county where the prosecution occurs is entitled to reimbursement for lodging, meals, and transportation. Since victims are almost always witnesses, they qualify for this reimbursement. The level of reimbursement is the same as that for a state employee. This level currently allows for expenses not to exceed $80 per night for lodging, $30 per day for meals, and $.25 per mile in a personal car.

To start the reimbursement process, the witness must complete a form listing expenses and must swear to its accuracy. Many counties advance these expenses, particularly for plane tickets. The state reimbursement process normally takes only a few weeks.

NOTICE TO EMPLOYERS Victims have a right to request that prosecutors notify their employers of the need for the victims to miss work to testify. Usually, prosecutors send a letter. Most employers are very understanding of the need for victims to miss work to testify.

VICTIM'S RIGHT TO PRIVACY Anyone may view the court's file, a public document, at the district or county clerk's office. However, the victim's address is excluded from this file unless it identifies the place of the crime, and a victim's phone number is never part of this file.

VICTIM IMPACT STATEMENT One of the significant ways a victim may impact the case is through the victim impact statement (VIS). The VIS is a ten-page form developed by the Texas Crime Victim Clearinghouse. The prosecutor's office mails it to violent crime victims within 10 days after defendants are indicted. The VIS allows victims to describe the physical, emotional, and economic consequences of the crime. It also asks whether or not they wish to be notified about the defendant's parole.

Many victims complete the VIS by themselves, whereas others need assistance or encouragement. In this area, the victim assistance coordinator or other victim advocate can make a real difference. It is not enough to simply mail the VIS to victims. The advocate needs to explain the importance of the VIS and encourage or help the victim to complete the form.

Victims return the VIS to the prosecutor's office. After judges find defendants guilty, they ask prosecutors for the VIS. Judges must also give the defense an opportunity for comment. (The front sheet of the VIS, which contains the address and phone number of the victim, is removed before the defense is allowed to examine the report.) Judges must consider the information in the VIS when sentencing defendants. After sentencing, the court forwards the VIS to the Institutional Division (for defendants sentenced to prison) or to the probation department (for defendants sentenced to probation).

PRE-SENTENCE REPORT Probation officers write pre-sentence reports, which describe the circumstances of the offense, the criminal and social history of the defendant, and a proposed sentencing plan. Victims have a right to provide information about the impact of the crime on themselves and their families. Probation officers will contact victims to obtain this information. Probation officers will also obtain information about the amount of financial restitution needed to adequately compensate victims for the crimes.

Judges may always request such reports in both felony and misdemeanor cases, but they are also required to order such reports in most felony cases.

Unless defendants consent, judges may not read pre-sentence reports until defendants are convicted. These reports are confidential and can be released only to prosecutors, defendants, and defendants' lawyers. The defense is entitled to read and respond to these reports.

For defendants sentenced to prison, the court clerk forwards the pre-sentence reports to the Institutional Division, which then forwards them to the Pardons and Paroles Division.

CHILD SAFETY ZONES A judge who places a child sex offender on probation or a parole panel that releases such an offender must create a child safety zone around the defendant. This child safety zone is a series of probation or parole conditions prohibiting defendants from being part of any athletic, civic, or cultural activity that involves children under the age of 18. These conditions prohibit defendants from going into or near places where children commonly gather, including schools, playgrounds, and video arcades. In addition, these conditions require defendants to receive counseling.

VICTIM STATEMENT AT SENTENCING Violent-crime victims are entitled to make a statement to the judge and defendant after sentencing. The statement may reflect the victims' views about the offense, the defendant, and the effect of the offense on the victim. The statement may not be recorded by the court reporter. It must be made after all elements of the sentence have been decided and after the sentence has been formally pronounced.

HATE CRIMES Special sentencing and parole rules apply when a defendant commits a hate crime. A hate crime is any crime where the victim is selected because of the defendant's bias or prejudice against that victim's group. If the judge or jury determines that a crime is a hate crime, the punishment range increases by one category unless it is a first-degree felony. For defendants sent to prison, release on parole or mandatory supervision must include 300 hours of community service work at a project serving primarily the victim or the group that was the defendant's target.

WHAT IS A HATE CRIME?

A hate crime is a crime motivated by prejudice or hatred toward the victim. Under federal law, state governments now keep statistics on murder, rape, robbery, aggravated assault, theft, motor vehicle theft, burglary, arson, simple assault, intimidation, and vandalism. Despite these reporting requirements, it is widely thought that hate crimes are significantly underreported. In 2003, 295 reported hate crimes in Texas involved 298 victims and 326 offenders.

The 2003 hate crime offenses broke down as follows:

Vandalism: 39%

Simple Assault: 20%

Intimidation: 22%

Aggravated Assault: 12%

Other: 7%

The leading motivations for the 2003 reported hate crimes were

Anti-Black: 42%

Anti-White: 7%

Anti-homosexual: 18%

Anti-Hispanic: 10%

Anti-Arab: 5%

Anti-Jewish: 7%

Anti-Asian: 3%

Other: 8%

PAROLE NOTIFICATION Upon request, a victim is entitled to be notified when the defendant is released or considered for parole. The victim simply checks a box on the victim impact statement. The victim can also communicate this request directly, by mail or phone, to the Texas Department of Criminal Justice Victim Services Division, which receives roughly 2,500 victim impact statements and sends approximately 20,000 victim notifications each year.

PAROLE PROTESTS In addition to the right of notification, victims are also entitled to provide information to the parole board before an inmate is considered for parole. This is a critical right for victims—one of the places in the system where victims can have a real impact. Victims have a chance to protest a parole; such protests can be very effective at keeping inmates locked up long past their initial parole eligibility dates.

Victims are not alone in having an opportunity to protest a parole. By law, the trial officials (judge, prosecutor, and sheriff) are notified of an upcoming parole decision. Often, one or more of these officials will register strong opposition to a parole.

Although not every parole protest is successful, many of them are. Carefully planned protests based upon objective facts have been enormously successful in keeping dangerous criminals locked up. Indeed, when I was district attorney my office identified roughly 100 of the most dangerous criminals from Williamson County, whom we believe should never be paroled. We obtained letters from victims, their friends and family, the investigating officers, and public officials each time one of the inmates was reviewed for parole; we then forwarded these letters to the parole board. We also made sure the parole board had a color photograph of the victim's injuries in each case where there were visible injuries. My successor, District Attorney John Bradley, has continued a similar effort. In the fourteen years of this effort, not one of our "100 worst" has been paroled.

PAROLE PROTESTS WORK

Some victims and other concerned citizens have organized letter writing and media attention campaigns to block a particular inmate's release on parole. In many cases, the protestors have succeeded.

• Genene Jones, a pediatric nurse who injected numerous babies at hospitals in San Antonio and Kerrville with Arectol—several of whom died before Jones was arrested in 1983—was the subject of the most highly publicized recent parole protest. She was ultimately convicted of two of the babies' deaths and given 99- and 60-year sentences. Due to a quirk in the law, which has since been corrected, she was eligible for parole after serving only 6 years. However, a victim-launched campaign, which produced 1,200 calls and letters to the parole board, resulted in denial of parole. At each later review her parole has again been denied. Her next review is scheduled for 2005.

• James Cross, who was convicted of the brutal rape and murder of two University of Texas coeds in 1965, was the subject of the most successful organized protest before his automatic release in 1992. (The law which required Cross's automatic release has since been changed; such a release would no longer be required.) In the end, Cross ended up serving 27 years of an 80-year sentence. During his incarceration, he was the subject of hundreds of protest letters and petitions organized by the former sorority of the two victims. He was reviewed for parole release 20 times; all 20 times parole was denied.

• Larry Ross and Selwynn Gholson, who during a 1974 bank robbery shot three people in the head in the small Central Texas town of Walburg and later murdered a highway patrolman in Bell County, are the focus of one of the longest-running active parole protests. The two killers were originally sentenced to death, but a U.S. Supreme Court ruling later changed those sentences to life in prison. Petitions and letters have flooded the parole board each time Ross and Gholson

are considered for release. Each time, they have been denied parole. Ross and Gholson have now each served 31 years in prison.

TOUGHER SENTENCING LAWS A discussion of specific crime victim laws would not be complete without mentioning the tougher sentencing laws passed during the 1993 legislative session. The significance of these changes cannot be overstated. Texas now has the toughest sentences for violent crimes of any state. The legislature

- expanded the 3g category (see p. 127) to include indecency with a child and all murders (sexual assault of a child was added in 1995)
- increased 3g time from 25% (up to 15 calendar years) to 50% (up to 30 calendar years) of sentence
- created the felony offense of intoxication assault, punishable by up to 10 years in prison (under the old law, this crime was frequently treated as a misdemeanor)
- doubled the maximum punishment for intoxication manslaughter from 10 years to 20 years

RESTITUTION TO VICTIMS

COURT-ORDERED RESTITUTION The law authorizes judges, as part of the sentence, to order that defendants pay restitution to their victims. If judges do not order restitution or order only partial restitution, they must state their reasons on the record. In a misdemeanor case, restitution replaces a fine.

Judges may order restitution for property loss or damage, for medical treatment of bodily injury, and for wages lost due to bodily injury. With the consent of the victim, the judge may order the defendant to perform services rather than pay money. Normally, the probation office collects restitution in monthly installments. If the offender has probation revoked or is sent directly to prison, parole or mandatory supervision conditions must include restitution payments.

When the defense disputes the amount of restitution, the trial judge must conduct a hearing. The prosecutor must prove the amount of restitution due by a preponderance of the evidence standard (which is a much easier standard to prove than the beyond a reasonable doubt standard).

Failure to pay restitution gives judges and parole boards grounds to revoke probation, parole, or mandatory supervision. Before revoking, they must consider the defendant's employment status, earning ability, and financial resources, along with the willfulness of the failure to pay and any other special circumstances.

Court-ordered restitution is very successful, reimbursing tens of millions of dollars to victims each year. However, it has drawbacks. It is available only when an offender is caught and convicted. The victim gets only small payments over many years. Also, prison inmates do not earn any money and so cannot pay any restitution.

CRIME VICTIMS COMPENSATION ACT In 1979, the legislature created the Crime Victims' Compensation (CVC) program. CVC reimburses eligible victims of violent crime for financial losses. The program is funded by fees that criminals pay as part of their sentences. In recent years, federal funds have expanded the program. CVC started slowly, with relatively few claims and payments. It has grown steadily. Today, CVC pays out approximately $70 million to roughly 11,000 crime victims annually.

$508,200,000 **in benefits has been paid to victims of violent crime through the Crime Victims' Compensation System.**

Source: Texas Attorney General's Office, Victims' Compensation 2003 Annual Report

Benefits Provided CVC pays benefits to eligible victims of violent crimes or to surviving spouses or children (eligibility and limitations are discussed below). CVC does not pay benefits to victims of nonviolent crimes and does not reimburse property loss or damage. CVC reimburses for

- medical, hospital, nursing, physical therapy or psychiatric care
- lost wages due to injury or court proceedings
- child care so a victim or victim's spouse can continue working
- crime scene clean-up (up to $750)
- replacement costs for clothing or bedding which was seized as evidence or rendered unusable by crime lab testing

For a deceased victim, CVC reimburses

- funeral and burial expenses
- loss of support to a dependent

- child care that enables a surviving spouse to work
- counseling for members of the immediate family

Eligibility Requirements Victims must meet several requirements to be eligible for CVC:

- The victims must be Texas residents, United States residents who become crime victims while in Texas, or Texas residents who become victims in a state with no CVC program.
- The victims must file the claim within one year of the crime. Exceptions include child victims.
- The crimes must be reported to law enforcement within 72 hours after the crime. Exceptions include child victims.
- The victims must cooperate fully with law enforcement and prosecution personnel.
- The victims must not have contributed to the crime by their own misconduct.
- The payment may not unjustly enrich a defendant or accomplice.
- The victims cannot have been inmates when the crime occurred.

Limitations on CVC Awards CVC awards are subject to certain limitations:

- Total recovery cannot exceed $25,000. An additional $25,000 can be awarded for catastrophic injuries. This money can be used only for making a home or automobile accessible, for job training or rehabilitation, for training in the use of special appliances, for home health care, or for reimbursement of lost wages.
- Lost wages cannot exceed $400 per week.
- Child care is limited to $100 per week per child.
- Loss of support to dependent family members cannot exceed $400 per week.

CVC pays benefits only to the extent that there is no other source for payment. Other sources include

- restitution from the defendant
- insurance: health, life, disability, or other
- employee benefits: workers' compensation, sick leave, wage continuation program

- government programs: Social Security, Medicare, Medicaid
- awards from a civil lawsuit

Filing Application Crime victims file a CVC application with the Texas attorney general's office. Law enforcement agencies must distribute application forms to eligible victims. Prosecutors' offices also have the forms. A victim can also obtain a form by writing to:

Texas Attorney General
Crime Victims' Compensation Division
P.O. Box 12548
Austin, Texas 78711-2548

Victims can also call the attorney general's office toll-free, 1–800–983–9933.

Verification Procedures The attorney general's office processes and investigates the application form. It currently takes that office about three months to act on an application and process claims for benefits. Although victims may hire a lawyer to handle the initial application, they can file almost all claims without one. About two thirds of all claims are approved. For over two thirds of the claims rejected, the reason for denial is that the victim shared responsibility for the offense or failed to cooperate with law enforcement.

There is an elaborate appeals process for denied claims. This process can include filing a lawsuit in court. A private lawyer must file such a lawsuit.

CRIME VICTIM ADVOCATES/INFORMATION SOURCES A large number of organizations and offices provide information or services to crime victims in Texas. These groups can be divided into two broad categories: those directly associated with a government entity and private groups. Many of the private groups receive some type of government grant.

GOVERNMENT PROGRAMS Some government victim programs are local programs mandated by the state. Others are funded by the state as part of a large agency's budget.

Law Enforcement–Based Programs Each law enforcement agency must have a crime victim liaison (CVL). The CVL assists violent crime victims either when they first contact the agency or as soon as possible thereafter. The CVL or responding officer gives the required information to victims. The CVL, along with the entire agency, must ensure that victims receive all of the rights guaranteed them by law.

Prosecutor-Based Programs District and county attorneys are all required to provide a victim assistance coordinator (VAC). Each person in the prosecutor's office, including the VAC, also makes sure that victims of violent crimes get all the services the law guarantees them. Many VACs provide additional services to victims of violent crimes; they also provide services to nonviolent crime victims.

A VAC must contact victims within 10 days of indictment or the filing of an information report. The VAC must inform victims of the various legal procedures and available programs. The VAC also forwards completed victim impact statements to the judge.

Texas Crime Victim Clearinghouse The Texas Crime Victim Clearinghouse is an agency run by the Texas Department of Criminal Justice (TDCJ) that maintains a toll-free number (1-800-252-3423) for general information or a referral on any topic relating to victims. It is an excellent source of information for anyone, professional or victim, who does not know where else to call.

The Clearinghouse sponsors an annual conference on victims' rights which provides education and technical support for hundreds of participants. The Clearinghouse also publishes a newsletter, the *Victim Assistance Resource Directory*, and conducts regional training sessions as needed throughout the state.

Victim Services Division The Victim Services Division of the TDCJ gives information to victims, allows them access to TDCJ personnel, and trains TDCJ personnel on victims' issues. Through the victims-only toll-free number (1-800-848-4284), the Victim Services Division gives victims information about inmates' status, including current parole eligibility dates, their prison assignments, their exact standing in the parole decision process, and restitution issues. This service is also a source for general information about parole and the corrections system. A new service of this division provides victims with an informational tour of a prison unit.

Victim Services notifies victims who request such information. Requests can be made in the victim impact statement or by calling the toll-free number. Victim Services then acknowledges the request and notifies the victim about the beginning of the parole review process as well as every decision made during the parole process. Victim Services also works with the Institutional Division so they can notify victims if the inmate escapes, is recaptured, is furloughed, or dies while in custody.

Texas was the first state with a Crime Stoppers program to operate behind the walls. The program runs much as conventional Crime Stoppers programs and includes cash rewards up to $1,000. In 2002, tips to the prison Crime Stoppers program helped solve 13 felony crimes, including 3 murders.

A victim/offender mediation or dialogue program also has been developed. It operates only on the request of the victim with the inmate's consent. Highly structured, it lets the victim meet face-to-face with the inmate. This meeting, in a secure, safe setting, is meant to help the victim recover from the trauma of the crime.

In addition, Victim Services is working with the Community Justice Assistance Division to develop victims' programs in local probation departments. One of these programs notifies victims when the offender

- is placed on probation
- is placed in a residential program
- is released from a residential program
- transfers to a new supervising probation officer
- requests early discharge (and the outcome of this request)
- is discharged from probation
- absconds
- is sentenced to jail
- has a motion to revoke probation filed
- has probation revoked

PRIVATE PROGRAMS Hundreds of private organizations—many funded by government grants—give information, referrals, or direct services to crime victims. The *Victim Assistance Resource Directory*, published by the Texas Crime Victim Clearinghouse, lists these organizations, many of which also seek to change the criminal justice system.

Statewide Advocacy Groups Statewide advocacy groups actively lobby the legislature to change the laws that affect victims. Many local chapters directly serve victims in their communities. Some of the better-known groups include Mothers Against Drunk Driving, People Against Violent Crime, the Texas Council on Family Violence, Justice for All, Texans for Equal Justice, and Parents of Murdered Children.

Rape Crisis Centers Most populated areas are covered by local rape crisis centers, which directly serve victims of sexual assault. These centers typically provide a crisis hotline, hospital and court accompaniment, peer and support groups, public education, prevention programs, and referrals to professional therapists.

Battered Women's Shelters At least 76 local women's shelters in Texas temporarily house victims of battering and their children. They also provide counseling, referrals, gas money, clothes, child care, and other services that battering victims may need.

No one wants to be a crime victim. It is, at best, a bad situation. But as this chapter has set out, crime victims are no longer ignored. They have very real rights which are being enforced every day. Whether it is the child abuse victim being taken to the children's advocacy center, the assault victim receiving a victim's compensation check, or the family of the murder victim completing a victim impact statement, crime victims are benefiting daily from rights and programs that were unheard of twenty-five years ago.

The final chapter will focus on the juvenile system. With headlines screaming about drive-by shootings, gang activities, and violent crimes being committed even by preteens, juvenile crime is an obvious concern to everyone.

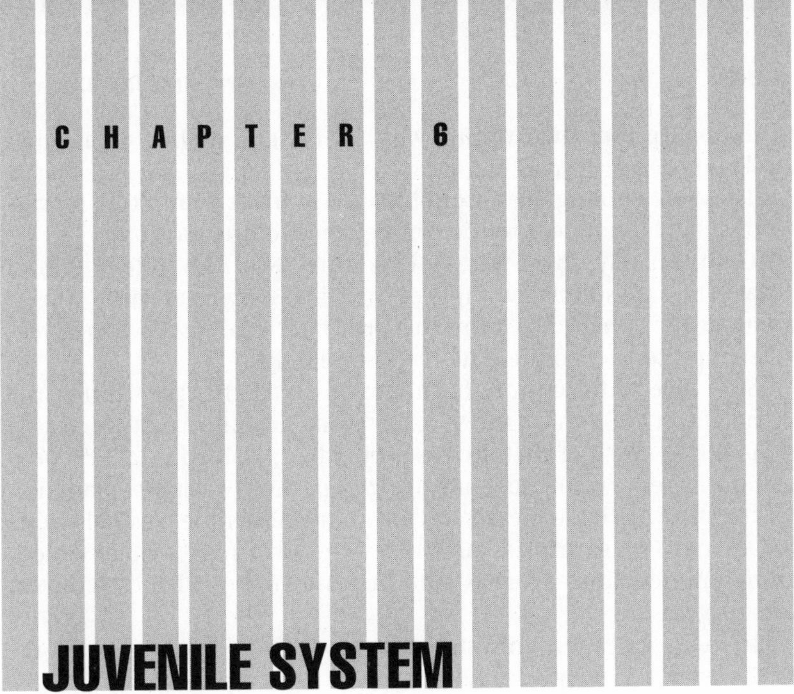

CHAPTER 6

JUVENILE SYSTEM

In the early 1990s, the juvenile crime situation mirrored the adult crime situation—it was out of control and getting worse. Yet with a few commonsense reforms and greatly increased incarceration capacity, juvenile crime came under control, just as adult crime did. Consider the following:

Item #1: On January 9, 1992, fifteen-year-old Stacey and her sixteen-year-old boyfriend Robert decided to run away from home. First, they stabbed Stacey's mother to death and then set out to drive to Alabama. Barely a hundred miles from home, they ran out of gas. With no money to buy gas, they waited in their car until the police came and apprehended them.

Item #2: On December 2, 1989, twelve-year-old Terrence invited the thirteen-year-old girl next door over to his house while his parents were away. He stabbed her 97 times, cleaned up the house, and placed her body under a woodpile. Later, he calmly helped search for her. The body was discovered the following day, and he was arrested shortly thereafter.

Item #3: On February 25, 1994, a sixteen-year-old boy went to his best friend's house, talked to his friend's mother about a social event, then took his friend out to a field where he shot him 23 times, reloading once, before leaving the dead body near a small creek. Later that weekend, he and his girlfriend went to his friend's house and asked the mother if she had seen her son. The body was discovered two days later. When he was arrested for the murder, he complained to the police that their timing was bad because he had a date that weekend.

These are chilling tales. Cold-blooded murders committed by kids who seemed indifferent to the consequences of their actions.

Unfortunately, these were not the three worst juvenile crimes in Texas. They are simply a sample of cases I was involved with. At least a half-dozen other cases from my own files were just as bad. Every veteran prosecutor in the state has a similar list.

Statewide statistics bore out these observed changes. During the decade from 1984 through 1993, statewide juvenile arrests increased 47%. While much of that increase could be explained by a 30% population increase in the juvenile age group, there was no explanation for the skyrocketing increases in violent juvenile crime. Overall arrests for violent crimes tripled. Arrests for the two most serious violent crimes, murder and sexual assault, increased threefold and eightfold, respectively.

In the face of these grim statistics, newly elected Governor George Bush made juvenile justice reform one of his top priorities. The legislature, meeting in 1995, responded with a number of positive reforms —particularly in terms of the system's ability to deal with the worst offenders. Several notable changes include

- lowering the age that the most serious offenders may be certified to stand trial as an adult from 15 to 14
- applying determinate sentencing to a much wider range of crimes
- continuing the expansion of the Texas Youth Commission from a 2,000-bed system to a 5,000-bed system
- limiting the discretion a juvenile probation department or intake officer used to have to simply dismiss criminal charges without a formal reason
- making juvenile hearings public unless a judge finds a specific reason to close them
- making it easier for law enforcement agencies to get information about juveniles from other agencies

Although these reforms, many of them long overdue, may not have radically changed the system, they nevertheless made the system work better. They are also helping isolate and punish more of the very worst juvenile offenders.

How well did these reforms work? Juvenile arrests for index crimes (murder, rape, robbery, aggravated assault, burglary, theft, and motor vehicle theft) peaked at 54,595 in 1994 and fell steadily to 30,949 in

2003. That's a decline of better than 40%. The statistics for murder were even better; they fell from 286 in 1994 to 50 in 2002—a whopping decline of 83%.

THE JUVENILE SYSTEM The juvenile system, which operates separately from the adult criminal system, deals with children who engage in certain types of improper conduct. This conduct can range from truancy to capital murder. A child subject to the juvenile system must be between the ages of 10 and 17 at the time of the conduct. Texas law does not provide for any legal consequences in the juvenile system for conduct committed before the 10th birthday. Juveniles are not technically charged with a crime. Instead, the two broad categories of juvenile misconduct are delinquent conduct and conduct indicating a need for supervision. Delinquent conduct includes

- all felonies
- Class A and B misdemeanors (except DWI)
- violation of certain juvenile, justice, or municipal court orders (except for truancy, running away, or Class C misdemeanors)

Conduct indicating a need for supervision (CINS) includes

- Class C misdemeanors
- truancy
- running away
- misdemeanor driving while intoxicated
- inhalant abuse
- certain school expulsions (such as for drug and firearm possession and for assault)
- conduct that violates a court-ordered condition of an at-risk child program

Also, a child can be prosecuted in the adult system for perjury and for traffic offenses.

144,667 juveniles were arrested in 2003—a 21% decrease from 1995.

Source: Texas Department of Public Safety

JUVENILE BOARDS Each county in Texas is served by one of 198 juvenile boards; some boards serve more than one county. The juvenile board is composed of the county judge, the district judges of the county, and the judges of any juvenile courts. Some counties, governed by special local laws, put a different, although similar, group on their board. The juvenile board

- appoints the chief juvenile probation officer
- sets policy and budget for the juvenile probation department
- designates which courts will hear juvenile cases

Juvenile boards also have other specific duties. For example, they annually inspect any juvenile detention facility and determine its suitability.

JUVENILE COURT The juvenile board designates the juvenile court or courts. The juvenile court can be any district or county court operating in the county. If a county court is designated, a district court must also be designated. The most serious juvenile cases—which have the possibility of a transfer of the juvenile to an adult prison—must be tried in a district court.

JUVENILE PROBATION DEPARTMENT A juvenile probation department has a chief, as many probation officers as needed, and a support staff. The juvenile probation office normally does intake of cases and sends a representative to all court proceedings. A juvenile probation officer must have a college degree and be certified by the state. Juvenile probation departments also operate any formal juvenile detention centers.

Texas has 161 juvenile probation departments, 48 of which serve multi-county areas. They employ more than 1,500 juvenile probation officers and more than 500 certified detention personnel.

TEXAS JUVENILE PROBATION COMMISSION The Texas Juvenile Probation Commission (TJPC) is a statewide agency governed by a nine-member board appointed by the governor and confirmed by the senate. The board is made up of two district judges, one county judge or commissioner, and six citizens (who may not be employed in the adult or juvenile systems). The TJPC

- oversees the local department
- certifies local officers
- channels state funding to local departments (state funding accounts for slightly more than 25% of local budgets)
- provides minimum standards for juvenile detention facilities

TEXAS YOUTH COMMISSION The Texas Youth Commission (TYC) is the state agency responsible for the juvenile corrections system. Much like the TJPC, the TYC is run by a six-member board appointed by the governor and confirmed by the senate.

The TYC operates a rapidly expanding 24-unit correctional system. Between 1995 and 1999, the TYC more than doubled its beds to a capacity of 5,200. The TYC currently operates a statewide reception center (Marlin); eleven correctional facilities, located in Brownwood, Gainesville, Crockett, Pyote, Giddings, Jefferson County, Mart, San Saba, Vernon; one residential treatment center for emotionally disturbed juveniles (Corsicana); a community residential facility (Edinburg); a boot camp (Sheffield); and nine halfway houses. The TYC also maintains a statewide contract system of various residences run by private operators.

JUVENILE PROCEDURE Juvenile procedure combines adult criminal law protections for defendants and various procedures designed to protect juveniles. In most cases, even when the procedure of the two systems is similar, they use different terminology.

CUSTODY A juvenile arrest is referred to as "a taking into custody." A juvenile may be taken into custody without a written arrest warrant whenever a law enforcement officer has reasonable grounds to believe the juvenile has engaged in delinquent conduct or conduct in need of supervision.

PLACE OF DETENTION When law enforcement officers take juveniles into custody and detain them, they may not take them to an adult jail. Instead, they must take juveniles to a detention center that is separate from any adult criminal facility. The detention center must be certified under state standards as being suitable for juveniles.

BOOKING Juveniles taken into custody are not routinely photographed and fingerprinted, although the juvenile court may authorize photographing or fingerprinting. Other exceptions allow photographing and fingerprinting for certain serious crimes and for investigative purposes.

DETENTION HEARING There is no bail in juvenile cases. Juveniles may be released to parents or other appropriate persons. Juveniles stay in detention only if

- they are likely not to appear for court
- they have no parent or other person able to return them to court

- they have no suitable care
- they may be dangerous to themselves or others
- they have a previous finding of delinquency or a conviction for a felony or a Class A or B misdemeanor

Juveniles must have a detention hearing before a judge within two working days of the offense. At the hearing, the judge must find one of the above five situations or must release the juvenile. New detention hearings must be held periodically but not more than 10 days apart until the juvenile is released or the case disposed of.

FORMAL CHARGES The juvenile system has an intake officer who is normally connected to the probation department. This officer's preliminary investigation determines whether

- the juvenile is a "child" within the juvenile system's age and offense definitions
- there is probable cause to believe the juvenile has committed either delinquent conduct or conduct in need of supervision

After this investigation, a prosecutor may file a petition, which has formal charges much like those in a misdemeanor information. Juveniles have no right to a grand jury indictment. The two-phase trial of a juvenile case proceeds much like that of an adult case. The determination-of-guilt phase is called the "adjudication hearing"; the punishment phase is called the "disposition hearing."

ADJUDICATION HEARING Juveniles are entitled to a jury at the adjudication hearing. They have all the normal adult trial rights, including the right to a lawyer, the presumption of innocence, the right to confront and cross-examine witnesses, and the right not to incriminate themselves.

The rules of evidence in juvenile and adult trials are virtually identical. A major exception is the written statement of a juvenile. For an adult, a law enforcement officer ordinarily gives the Miranda warnings. However, juveniles must have a judge give them a juvenile version of the warnings before a written statement may be taken. Also, juveniles must sign the statement in the judge's presence; no law enforcement officers or personnel from the prosecutor's office may be present.

DISPOSITION HEARING The disposition hearing is similar to the punishment phase of the adult criminal process, with one exception. Juveniles generally have no right to a jury. In order to impose a disposition on juvenile offenders, the judge must first find that either the juveniles need rehabilitation or that the protection of the public or the juveniles requires a disposition. The judge has a wide range of options, including probation or an indeterminate commitment to the TYC.

A juvenile court disposition may also order family members to receive counseling or certain individuals not to have contact with the juvenile. In addition, juvenile courts can suspend a juvenile's driver's license, regardless of the offense committed.

RECORDS AND FILES Juvenile files and records of the court and the prosecutor are open only to the judge, probation officers, lawyers, and agencies providing supervision or custody. They are not open to the public. The judge may give access to anyone else with a legitimate reason on a case-by-case basis.

PUBLIC ACCESS Laws passed in 1995 reverse the presumption that juvenile hearings should be closed to the public. All juvenile court proceedings are public unless the court excludes the public for good cause. Even if the judge orders the hearing closed, the victim may still attend the hearing unless the court finds that the victim is to testify and that the victim's testimony would be materially affected by hearing the other testimony at the trial.

PARENTAL ATTENDANCE Parents, including conservators, custodians, or guardians, must attend all court proceedings. The judge may exempt a person for good cause. There is also an exception for nonresidents of Texas. Failure to attend such a hearing can be punished by a fine of up to $1,000 for contempt of court. An employer must give such a person time off from work to attend the hearing and may not fire a worker because of such attendance.

DISPOSITION

CERTIFICATION A juvenile court may certify juveniles to stand trial as adults for any felony offense if they were 15 or 16 years old at the time of the offense. Certification means that the juvenile courts waive their jurisdiction and the juvenile is transferred to adult criminal courts. Juveniles who were 14 at the time of the offense may be certified for capital murder, an aggravated controlled-substance felony, or any first-degree felony. Once certified, a juvenile remains certified for all future conduct.

The court must conduct special hearings to determine whether it is appropriate to certify juveniles. If the court does certify, the prosecutor's office must present the cases to grand juries to begin formal adult procedures. Once certified, juveniles transfer to adult jails. They serve any sentences, including prison, in the adult system.

177 juveniles were certified to stand trial as adults in 2002. This figure represents a steady decrease from 1994, when 596 juveniles were certified.

Source: Texas Juvenile Probation Commission

DETERMINATE SENTENCING A hybrid of juvenile and adult law, determinate sentencing lets juveniles tried in the juvenile system receive fixed sentences. If the sentences include confinement, the juveniles go to the TYC with a possibility for transfer to the adult system at age 18. Determinate sentencing punishes the most serious and dangerous felonies:

- murder and capital murder
- aggravated kidnapping
- sexual assault, aggravated sexual assault, and indecency with a child
- aggravated robbery
- aggravated assault, felony deadly conduct, and serious assaults on children, the elderly, and the disabled
- first-degree drug offenses
- attempts to commit murder, capital murder, aggravated robbery, aggravated sexual assault, indecency with a child, and aggravated kidnapping

Habitual juvenile offenders—those who have committed a serious felony after two prior felony adjudications—may also be subject to the determinate sentencing law. To trigger the determinate sentencing law, prosecutors take the juvenile petitions to grand juries. The grand jurors may approve or disapprove the petitions. If they approve, the cases return to juvenile court where the juveniles then receive determinate sentences. The only procedural difference is that the juveniles have a right to have juries set sentences at the disposition hearings. At the disposition hearings, the court or jury may assess either probation or confinement. The confinement can be no longer than

- 40 years for a capital felony, a first-degree felony, or an aggravated controlled-substance felony
- 20 years for a second-degree felony
- 10 years for a third-degree felony

If juveniles are committed under determinate sentencing, they are first sent to the TYC. They may be released on parole by the TYC at any time after the following minimum sentences have been served:

capital murder—10 years
first-degree felony—3 years
second-degree felony—2 years
third-degree felony—1 year

If juveniles are not paroled and do not complete their sentences, the TYC must refer them back to the original juvenile courts for transfer or release hearings. To trigger these hearings

- the TYC makes the referral to juvenile court for the purposes of transferring the juveniles to adult prison. This referral requires that
  - the juveniles be between ages 16 and 21
  - the juveniles' conduct indicates that the welfare of the community requires a transfer to the Institutional Division
- The TYC makes the referral to juvenile court for the purposes of releasing juveniles under supervision. The TYC can make this request at any time.

If such transfer or release hearings are held, the juveniles have a full array of trial rights: to have a lawyer, to cross-examine witnesses, to present evidence. The juveniles do not have the right to a jury. Juveniles still in TYC custody when they turn 21 will automatically be released on adult parole. If they are released on supervision either by the TYC or the juvenile court after they turn 19, they are also released on adult parole. Once on adult parole, they are supervised the same as any other adult. If their parole is later revoked, they are sent to an adult prison.

JUVENILE ADJUDICATION A judge has a third option: to proceed entirely under the juvenile system. First, juveniles have adjudication hearings. If the hearings find that the juveniles engaged in delinquent conduct or conduct indicating a need for supervision, they have disposition hearings.

The procedure for disposition hearings is the same as that for the adjudication hearings—the juveniles have the right to a lawyer, to cross-examine witnesses, and to present evidence. They have no right to a jury. The court may either place them on probation or commit them for an indefinite term to the TYC.

Most often, juveniles are placed on probation in their own homes. If the court finds that they cannot receive the care, support, and supervision needed to meet the conditions of probation, the court may place them in some alternative such as a foster home or a group home run by a private agency. The court may place juveniles found guilty of delinquent conduct in an intermediate sanction facility.

The court can impose any reasonable condition on juveniles' probation. The court must impose community service work, not to exceed 500 hours, unless exceptional circumstances (such as physical handicap) prevent it. The court fixes the length of probation for any term deemed appropriate. However, the juveniles must complete it by their 18th birthday. The court also has broad powers to order that

- the juveniles' driver's licenses be suspended
- other individuals stop acts which contribute to the delinquency of the juveniles
- the parents pay restitution or perform community service work

If the parents can show a good faith effort to prevent their child's conduct, the court should not impose restitution or community service. Juveniles who violate a condition of probation have a hearing to modify the disposition. The court may change the conditions of probation or commit the juveniles to the TYC.

If the juveniles engaged in delinquent conduct, the court may make a direct commitment to the TYC at the adjudication hearing. Any such commitment is for an indeterminate time. That is, the TYC determines the release date by paroling the juveniles. They must be released if not paroled by their 18th birthday.

Juveniles guilty of conduct indicating a need for supervision may not be sent directly to the TYC. However, if they violate a condition of their probation, they may be sent to the TYC.

DEFERRED PROSECUTION Some juvenile cases may proceed without a formal referral to juvenile court. A juvenile probation department, juvenile prosecutor, or juvenile judge may place a juvenile on deferred prosecution. However, the juvenile probation department may not place juveniles on deferred prosecution if they

- allegedly committed a felony or a misdemeanor involving violence or a deadly weapon
- have a prior felony adjudication

A prosecutor may place any juveniles on deferred prosecution, including those who cannot be given a deferred prosecution by a juvenile probation department.

Deferred prosecutions are a form of informal probation. Restitution—both financial to the victim and service to the community—is frequently part of the deferred prosecution. A period of detention may not be required. Such a disposition is strictly voluntary; the juveniles and their parents must agree to it. If the juveniles fail to successfully complete the deferred prosecution, the prosecutor can refer the original case to juvenile court.

INFORMAL DISPOSITIONS A law enforcement officer may also make an informal disposition of juvenile cases, to which the juveniles and their families must consent. Both local juvenile boards and the legislature, through the First Offenders Program, have set guidelines for this procedure. Under either set of guidelines, the officer disposes of the case without a referral to the juvenile system. Instead, the officer may refer juveniles to a youth intervention services program such as family counseling or mentoring. The guidelines can also require voluntary restitution and community service.

Despite the good news about dramatic reductions in juvenile crime, it remains a serious concern to us all. We need to continue protecting ourselves from violent predators—regardless of their age. But we also need to redirect the lives of as many young offenders as possible.

JUVENILE JUSTICE AT WORK

"Samantha," a 15-year-old girl, stood in front of my bench for a routine detention hearing, the kind I do several hundred times each year. Her mother had died in a car wreck a couple of years earlier; her father was an alcoholic who was in and out of jails. The child was before me as the result of a year of habitual truancy. The school and justice of the peace court had tried but failed to make the situation better, so they referred her case to juvenile court—to me. I had no real choice. There was no way I could release her to her father so I ordered her to be held in our detention center for at least 10 working days.

Samantha had had a tough year but she wasn't broken.

Just a couple of nights of good food and sleep at our detention center and her sparkling personality was already showing through. I asked the juvenile probation department to find some safe place for Samantha to live. They spent several weeks looking but finally came up with a grandmother in Wyoming. The grandmother was willing to take her, and it seemed like Samantha's best hope. We arranged for plane fare, my court staff brought some decent clothes from their own daughters' closets, and we sent Samantha on her way with more than one of us praying that things would work out.

Two months later we got a copy of her first report card. Samantha was taking a full load of college-prep classes—Algebra II, Biology, Spanish I, and so on—and her grades, seven A's and one B, were outstanding. But the teacher's comment, "A pleasure to have in class," is what really brought a tear to my eye.

Most juveniles can't be turned around like Samantha. Sometimes progress is measured by keeping a kid off drugs and in school for six months. Sometimes, if only for a few months, you provide safety from an adult world that is quick to exploit kids. But Texas has committed a lot of resources to getting delinquents headed in the right direction. Progress is made in juvenile court. The end result is that some kids do respond, and as a result Texas becomes a safer, better place for us all.

APPENDIX

TABLE OF CRIMES AND PUNISHMENTS

	(dollar amounts = maximum optional fine)
CF = capital felony	life imprisonment or death penalty
F1 = first-degree felony	5–99 years or life; $10,000
F2 = second-degree felony	2–20 years; $10,000
F3 = third-degree felony	2–10 years; $10,000
SJF = state jail felony	½–2 years; $10,000
A = Class A misdemeanor	up to 1 year or $4,000 or both
B = Class B misdemeanor	up to 180 days or $2,000 or both
C = Class C misdemeanor	$500
VL = value ladder	punishment based upon value of property involved (see chart p. 89)

Other abbreviations:
bi = bodily injury
sbi = serious bodily injury

Crime	*Penal Code*	*Punishment Range*
Abandoning Child (with intent to return)	22.041	SJF
Abandoning Child (without intent to return)	22.041	F3

Crime	Penal Code	Punishment Range
Abandoning Child (imminent danger)	22.041	F2
Absence from Community Corrections Facility, Unauthorized	38.113	SJF
Abuse of Corpse	42.08	A
Abuse of Official Capacity (misapplies property)	39.02	VL
Abuse of Official Capacity (violates law)	39.02	A
Academic Product, Deceptive Preparation/Marketing	32.50	C
Advertisement for Placement of a Child	25.09	A
Alcoholic Beverage in Motor Vehicle, Possession of	49.031	C
Amusement Ride, Assembling or Operating While Intoxicated	49.065	B
Arrest, Evading	8.04	B
Arrest, Evading (sbi)	38.04	F3
Arrest, Resisting	38.03	A
Arrest, Resisting (with deadly weapon)	38.03	F3
Arson	28.02	F2
Arson (bi or death)	28.02	F1
Assault (threat or contact)	22.01(a)(2)(3)	C
Assault (bi)	22.01(a)(1)	A
Assault, Aggravated	22.02	F2
Assault, Aggravated (public servant or retaliation)	22.02(b)	F1
Attack on Assistance Animal	42.091	A
Attack on Assistance Animal (injury)	42.091	SJF
Attack on Assistance Animal (death)	42.091	F3
Attempt, Criminal	15.01	One degree lower than offense attempted
Bad Check, Issuance of	32.41	B or C
Bail Jumping (C)	38.10	C
Bail Jumping (B or A)	38.10	A
Bail Jumping (felony)	38.1	F3

Crime	Penal Code	Punishment Range
Battery	38.12	A
Bigamy	25.01	A
Breach of Computer Security	33.02	A
Breach of Computer Security	33.02	VL
Bribery, Commercial	32.43	SJF
Bribery	36.02	F2
Burglary—Coin-Operated Machine	30.03	A
Burglary—Vehicle	30.04	A
Burglary—Vehicle (rail car)	30.04	SJF
Burglary—Building	30.02	SJF
Burglary—Habitation (theft)	30.02	F2
Burglary—Habitation (felony other than theft)	30.02	F1
Child, Endangering	22.041	SJF
Child, Enticing	25.04	B or F3
Child, Harboring Runaway	25.06	A
Child, Leaving in Vehicle	22.10	C
Child, Sale or Purchase of	25.08	F3
Child Pornography, Possession or Promotion of	43.26	F3
Cigarettes, Prohibitions Relating to Certain	48.015	A
Civil Rights of Person in Custody, Violation of	39.04	A or SJF
Coercion of Public Servant/Voter	36.03	A
Coercion of Public Servant/Voter (threat to commit felony)	36.03	F3
Communications, Sale or Distribution of Device	16.02	SJF
Communications, Unlawful Interception of (interference with lawful government interception)	16.02	SJF
Communications, Unlawful Interception of	16.02	F2
Communications, Public, Illegal Divulgence of (cellular phone)	16.05	C
Communications, Public, Illegal Divulgence of (intent to gain benefit)	16.05	A
Communications, Public, Illegal Divulgence of	16.05	SJF

Crime	*Penal Code*	*Punishment Range*
Communications, Stored, Unlawful Access to	16.04	A
Communications, Stored, Unlawful Access to (obtain benefit or harm another)	16.04	SJF
Credit Card Transaction Laundering	32.35	VL
Credit/Debit Card Abuse	32.31	SJF
Criminal Street Gang, Soliciting Membership	71.022	F3
Cruelty to Animals	42.09	A or SJF
Conspiracy, Criminal	15.02	One degree lower than offense attempted
Custody, Child, Interference with	25.03	SJF
Custody, Agreement to Abduct from	25.031	SJF
Deadly Conduct	22.05(a)	A
Deadly Conduct (knowing discharge of firearm at person, habitation, etc.)	22.05(b)	F3
Deceptive Business Practice	32.42	A or C
Disorderly Conduct	42.01	C
Disorderly Conduct (display or discharge of firearm)	42.01	B
Disrupting Meeting or Procession	42.05	B
Dog Fighting (spectator)	42.10	C
Dog Fighting	42.10	A
Dog Fighting (profits from or owns property where fight held)	42.10	SJF
Driving, Boating, or Flying While Intoxicated	49.04	B (72-hour minimum)
Driving, Boating, or Flying While Intoxicated (2nd offense)	49.04	A (15-day minimum)
Driving, Boating, or Flying While Intoxicated (3rd offense)	49.04	F3
Driving While Intoxicated with Child Passenger	49.045	SJF
Employment Harmful to Children	43.251	A
Endless Chain Scheme	32.48	B
Escape	38.06	A
Escape (bi)	38.06	F2

Crime	Penal Code	Punishment Range
Escape (felony or secure correctional facility)	38.06	F3
Escape (sbi or deadly weapon)	38.06	F1
Escape, Permitting or Facilitating	38.07	A
Escape, Permitting or Facilitating (felony or secure correctional facility)	38.07	F3
Escape, Permitting or Facilitating (deadly weapon or post-felony conviction)	38.07	F2
Evidence, Unlawful Interception of	37.09	F3
Explosives, Possession of Components of	46.09	F3
Failure to Identify (fugitive)	38.02	A or B
Failure to Identify (self)	38.02	B or C
Failure to Provide Notice and Report of Death of Resident of Institution	38.19	B
Failure to Report Death of Prisoner	39.05	B
Failure to Report a Felony	38.171	A
False Alarm or Report	42.06	A
False Alarm or Report (school or public utility)	42.06	SJF
False Identification as Peace Officer	37.12	B
False Report to Peace Officer	37.08	B
False Statement to Obtain Property or Credit	32.32	VL
Falsely Holding Oneself Out as a Lawyer	38.122	F3
Financing Statement, Fraudulent Filing	37.101	A or F3
Flag, Destruction of	42.11	A
Forgery	32.21	A
Forgery (commercial instrument)	32.21	SJF
Forgery (government document)	32.21	F3
Fraudulent Court, Record of	37.13	A
Fraudulent Destruction, Removal, or Concealment of a Writing (will, deed, or security agreement)	32.47	A or SJF
Fraudulent Transfer of Motor Vehicle (failure to disclose)	32.34	A

Crime	*Penal Code*	*Punishment Range*
Fraudulent Transfer of Motor Vehicle (<$20,000)	32.34	SJF
Fraudulent Transfer of Motor Vehicle ($20,000+)	32.34	F3
Gambling	47.02	C
Gambling Device, Possession of	47.06	A
Gambling Information, Communicating	47.07	A
Gambling Place, Keeping a	47.04	A
Gambling Promotion	47.03	A
Gang Membership, Coercing, Soliciting or Inducing	22.015	SJF or F3
Gift to Public Servant	36.08	A
Gift to Public Servant, Offering	36.09	A
Graffiti	28.08	VL
Harassment	42.07	B
Harassment by Persons/Correctional Facilities	22.11	F3
Harmful Material, Sale, Distribution, or Display of, to Minor	43.24	A
Harmful Material, Sale, Distribution, or Display of, to Minor (employs minor)	43.24	F3
Hindering Apprehension	38.05	A
Hindering Apprehension (felony)	38.05	F3
Hindering Secured Creditor	32.33	VL
Hindering Proceedings by Disorderly Conduct	38.13	A
Hoax Bombs	46.08	A
Honorarium, Acceptance of	36.07	A
Human Organs, Purchase or Sale of	48.02	A
Identifying Information/Fraudulent Use or Possession	32.51	SJF
Impersonating Public Servant	37.11	F3
Implements of Escape, Possession of	38.09	F3
Implements of Escape, Possession of (deadly weapon)	38.09	F2
Improper Contact with Victim	38.111	A or F3
Improper Influence	36.04	A
Improper Photography/Visual Recording	21.15	SJF

Crime	*Penal Code*	*Punishment Range*
Improper Relationship Between Educator/Student	21.12	F2
Indecency with Child (exposure)	21.11(a)(2)	F3
Indecency with Child (contact)	21.11(a)(1)	F2
Indecent Exposure	21.08	B
Injury to Child, Elderly, or Disabled Individual (reckless bi)	22.04	SJF
Injury to Child, etc. (negligent sbi)	22.04	SJF
Injury to Child, etc. (intentionally or knowingly causing bi)	22.04	F3
Injury to Child, etc. (reckless sbi)	22.04	F2
Injury to Child, etc. (intentionally or knowingly causing sbi)	22.04	F1
Interference with Emergency Telephone Call	42.062	A
Interference with Police Service Animals	38.151	Varies, C–F3
Interference with Public Duties	38.15	B
Interference with Rights of Guardian	25.10	SJF
Intoxication, Public	49.02	C
Intoxication Assault	49.07	F3
Intoxication Manslaughter	49.08	F2
Kidnapping	20.03	F3
Kidnapping, Aggravated (voluntary safe release)	20.04(c)	F2
Kidnapping, Aggravated	20.04	F1
Lewdness, Public	21.07	A
Manslaughter	19.04	F2
Misapplication of Fiduciary Property	32.45	VL
Mischief, Criminal	28.03	VL
Missing Child/Person, False Report	37.081	C
Money Laundering ($3,000–<$20,000)	34.02	F3
Money Laundering ($20,000–<$100,000)	34.02	F2
Money Laundering ($100,000+)	34.02	F1
Murder (sudden passion)	19.02(d)	F2
Murder	19.02(b)	F1
Murder, Capital	19.03	CF
Negligent Homicide, Criminally	19.05	SJF
Non-Support, Criminal	25.05	SJF

Crime	Penal Code	Punishment Range
Obscene Display	43.22	C
Obscenity	43.23	A
Obscenity (child under 18)	43.23	SJF
Obscenity (wholesale promotion)	43.23	SJF
Obscenity (wholesale promotion child under 18)	43.23	F3
Obstructing Highway	42.03	B
Obstruction/Retaliation	36.06	F3
Obstruction/Retaliation (juror victim)	36.06	F2
Official Information, Misuse of	39.06	F3
Official Oppression	39.03	A
Organized Criminal Activity	71.02	One degree higher than most serious offense planned or committed
Perjury	37.02	A
Perjury, Aggravated	37.03	F3
Possession of a Firearm, Unlawful	46.04	A or F3
Possession, Manufacture or Distribution of Certain Instruments Used to Commit Retail Theft	31.15	A
Practice of Law, Unauthorized	38.123	A
Prohibited Substance in Correctional Facility	38.11	F3
Prostitution	43.02	B
Prostitution, Promotion of	43.03	A
Prostitution, Aggravated Promotion	43.04	F3
Prostitution, Compelling	43.05	F2
Protective Order, Violation of	25.07	A
Railroad Property, Interference with	28.07	VL, with some exceptions
Reckless Damage or Destruction	28.04	C
Recruitment of Athlete, Illegal	32.441	VL
Refusal to Execute Release of Fraudulent Lien/Claim	32.49	A
Rigging of Publicly Exhibited Contest	32.44	A
Riot	42.02	B
Robbery	29.02	F2

Crime	*Penal Code*	*Punishment Range*
Robbery, Aggravated	29.03	F1
Sale/Multichannel Video or Information Services	31.14	A
Securing Execution of Document by Deception	32.46	VL
Sexual Assault	22.011	F2
Sexual Assault, Aggravated	22.021	F1
Sexual Conduct, Prohibited (incest)	25.05	F3
Sexual Performance by a Child	43.25	F2
Sexual Performance by a Child (produces or promotes)	43.25	F3
Silent or Abuse Calls to 911	42.061	B
Simulating Legal Process	32.48	A
Simulation, Criminal	32.22	A
Smoking Tobacco in an Illegal Place	48.01	C
Solicitation (of capital or first-degree felony), Criminal	15.03	One degree lower than offense solicited
Stalking	42.072	F3
Stolen Check/Sight Order, Stealing or Receiving	32.24	A
Suicide, Aiding	22.08	C
Suicide, Aiding (death or sbi)	22.08	SJF
Tampering with Consumer Product (threat)	22.09	F3
Tampering with Consumer Product	22.09	F2
Tampering with Consumer Product (sbi)	22.09	F1
Tampering with Government Record	37.10	A, F3 or F2
Tampering with Government Record (intent to defraud)	37.10	SJF
Tampering with Government Record (license)	37.10	F3
Tampering with Government Record (license with intent)	37.10	F2
Tampering with Identification Numbers	31.11	A
Tampering with Witness	36.05	SJF
Telecommunications Access Device, Publication of	33A.05	A

Crime	*Penal Code*	*Punishment Range*
Telecommunications Device, Manufacture, Possession, Delivery	33A.03	F3
Telecommunications Services, Theft	33A.04	VL
Telecommunications Services, Unauthorized Use	33A.02	VL
Terroristic Threat	22.07	B
Terroristic Threat (family violence or public servant)	22.07	A
Terroristic Threat (interrupt occupation)	22.07	A
Terroristic Threat (interrupt public service)	22.07	F3
Theft	31.03	VL
Theft/Multichannel Video or Information Services	31.12	C or A
Theft of Service	31.04	VL
Theft of Trade Secrets	31.05	F3
Tracking Device, Unlawful Installation	16.06	A
Trademark Counterfeiting	32.23	VL
Trafficking of Persons	20A.02(a)	F2
Trafficking of Persons (death or victim <14 for prostitution or obscenity)	20A.02(b)	F1
Trespass, Criminal	30.05	B
Trespass, Criminal (habitation, shelter center)	30.05	A
Trespass by Holder of License to Carry Concealed Handgun	30.06	A
Unlawful Restraint	20.02	A
Unlawful Restraint (victim under 17)	20.02	SJF
Unlawful Restraint (victim peace officer, risk of sbi or defendant in custody at time of restraint)	20.02	F3
Use of Accident Report Information, Pecuniary Gain	38.18	B
Use of a Criminal Instrument, Unlawful	16.01	One degree lower than offense intended

Crime	*Penal Code*	*Punishment Range*
Use of a Criminal Instrument, Unlawful (sale or manufacture)	16.01	SJF
Use of Laser Pointers	42.13	C
Use of Pen Register or Trap and Trace Device, Unlawful	16.03	SJF
Use of a Vehicle, Unauthorized	31.07	SJF
Violation of Protective Order Issued on Basis of Sexual Assault	38.112	A
Violation of Protective Order Preventing Hate Crime	25.071	A
Weapon, Carrying, in a Prohibited Place	46.03	F3
Weapon, Carrying Unlawfully	46.02	A
Weapon, Carrying Unlawfully (licensed premises)	46.02	F3
Weapon, Deadly, in Penal Institution	46.10	F3
Weapon, Taking or Attempting to Take from Peace Officer	38.14	SJF
Weapon, Prohibited, Possession of (switchblade or knuckles)	46.05	A
Weapon, Prohibited, Possession of	46.05	F3
Weapons, Unlawful Transfer of	46.06	A or SJF

GLOSSARY

acquittal: a finding of not guilty.

adjudication hearing: the proceeding in court to determine whether a juvenile is guilty of improper conduct. This hearing is the juvenile system's equivalent of a trial. See also *hearing*.

affirm: the ruling of an appeals court that upholds a conviction and sentence.

appeal: the process of asking another court to review a trial court's guilty verdict. The object of an appeal is to obtain a new trial or a not-guilty finding from the other court. The prosecutor and the victim do not have a right to appeal a not-guilty verdict.

appellate court: the court that reviews what happened in the trial court to determine whether the trial court followed the law.

arrest: the process of a law enforcement officer placing a suspect in custody.

arrest warrant: the written document from a magistrate authorizing a law enforcement officer to arrest a suspect.

Automated Fingerprint Identification System (AFIS): computerized system that allows law enforcement officers to take a fingerprint from a crime scene and determine whether it belongs to anyone whose fingerprints are on file within the state. See also *Combined DNA Index System (CODIS)*.

bail: the dollar amount which defendants must give as security that they will appear in court. Guaranteeing this dollar amount entitles the defendants to release from jail. See also *bond*.

bailiff: the officer who maintains order in the courtroom. Typically, a bailiff announces the court into session, escorts witnesses to the stand, and shepherds the jury into and out of the courtroom.

battered women's shelter: temporary housing for victims of battering and their children.

bench trial: the type of trial in which a judge (instead of a jury) determines guilt or innocence. Both the prosecutor and the defendant must agree to waive a jury trial before the judge can hear the case.

beyond a reasonable doubt: the legal requirement that evidence be of such a convincing character that a person would be willing to rely and act upon it without hesitation in the most important of his or her affairs. The prosecution must prove all criminal cases beyond a reasonable doubt. See also *preponderance of the evidence.*

bifurcated trial: the division of a jury trial into two parts—a guilt phase and a punishment phase. Evidence of prior convictions and other bad acts by defendants are not allowed in the guilt phase but are permitted in the punishment phase.

Bill of Rights: the first 10 amendments to the United States Constitution. These amendments prohibit unreasonable searches and seizures and guarantee trial by jury with representation by a lawyer and various other rights for criminal defendants. The Texas Constitution includes a similar list of guarantees for defendants. See also *Crime Victims' Bill of Rights.*

blood alcohol concentration (BAC): the amount of alcohol in an individual's blood. An individual with a BAC of .08 is considered legally intoxicated.

bond: the written agreement of a defendant to appear in court and abide by any other conditions set by the judge. It sometimes includes payment of cash or another security that is refundable if the defendant makes all court appearances. See also *bail, personal bond,* and *surety bond.*

boot camp: the secure facility that features military-style discipline along with rigorous work and exercise.

Brady motion: the legal document filed by the defense lawyer which asks the judge to order the prosecutor to disclose to the defense lawyer any evidence which might show that defendants did not commit the crimes or that they should get a lesser punishment. Brady was the defendant in the U.S. Supreme Court case that requires prosecutors to give such evidence to defense attorneys.

brief: the written argument filed by the defense lawyer with an appeals court. It sets out reasons why the appeals court should grant a new trial or not-guilty verdict. The prosecutor's written response is also called a brief. Briefs are not necessarily short; they are normally subject to a limit of 50 pages.

burden of proof: the legal requirement that prosecutors bring forward evidence to prove guilt. Defendants are not required to prove that they are not guilty.

capias: the order of a court to arrest a suspect.

capital murder: murder for which the possible punishment includes the death penalty.

cash bond: the payment to the court of all or part of the dollar amount of the bail. Cash bonds are fully refunded to the people who deposited the money if the defendants appear for all of their court dates.

certification: the process for juvenile courts to waive their jurisdiction and allow juveniles to be transferred to adult criminal courts. Any 15- or 16-year-old can be certified for committing a felony crime. Any 14-year-old can be certified for capital murder, aggravated controlled-substance felonies, and any first-degree felony.

challenge for cause: the right of both the prosecutor and the defense lawyer to ask that the judge excuse a potential juror for a specific reason. The reason usually has to do with a bias or prejudice against the defendant or the law that would make the potential juror unable to be fair in a particular case.

city attorney: the appointed city official who prosecutes traffic and other minor offenses in the city courts.

civil law: the group of laws that regulate noncriminal matters such as contracts, wills, corporations, and unintentional injuries.

clerk: the officer responsible for keeping all legal documents which are filed as part of a case. Typically, the clerk administers oaths to witnesses. (Sometimes the judge administers them.)

closing statement: the oral argument for a guilty or not-guilty verdict made by the prosecutor or defense lawyer at the end of a trial. See also *opening statement.*

code of criminal procedure: the collection of the major rules for investigations, arrests, trials, and punishments. The rules are passed by the Texas Legislature.

Combined DNA Index System (CODIS): computerized system that allows samples of known offenders' DNA to be matched with DNA from the scene of the unsolved crime. See also *Automated Fingerprint Identification System (AFIS); National DNA Index System (NDIS).*

community corrections facility (CCF): the residential facility designed to house probationers. Texas has six types of CCFs: restitution centers, court residential treatment facilities, substance abuse treatment facilities, boot camps, facilities for the mentally impaired, and intermediate sanction facilities.

community service: the requirement of probation that the probationer provide unpaid labor for a not-for-profit organization or government agency.

community supervision: the official name given probation in Texas. See also *probation.*

Community Supervision and Corrections Department (CSCD): the part of the Texas Department of Criminal Justice that supervises adult probation, much as the Pardons and Paroles Division supervises parolees. In all, Texas has 119 local CSCDs. See also *Texas Department of Criminal Justice.*

competence to stand trial: the legal requirement that defendants have enough mental capacity for a very basic understanding of the trial proceeding and for communicating with their lawyers. If defendants are not competent to stand trial, they can be committed to mental institutions until they are competent.

complaint: the sworn, written document that charges someone with committing a crime.

concurrent sentence: the practice of allowing additional sentences to be served at the same time as an earlier sentence. The sentencing judge determines whether sentences run concurrently or consecutively.

conduct indicating a need for supervision (CINS): the broad category of juvenile misconduct that is less serious than delinquent conduct. Class C misdemeanors, truancy, and running away are examples of CINS. See also *delinquent conduct.*

confession: the statement by which defendants admit that they committed crimes.

consecutive sentence: the practice of allowing additional sentences to be served only and immediately after a sentence from an earlier trial has been completed. The sentencing judge determines whether sentences run concurrently or consecutively.

consent search: the search agreed to by the person who legally controls the property. For this search, the law enforcement officers do not need a search warrant.

continuance: the postponement of a court hearing or trial.

Controlled Substances Act: the collection of the drug laws and their punishments. These laws are passed by the Texas Legislature.

count: the specific crime charged in a separate portion of an indictment or information, which can contain many counts.

county attorney: the elected county official who prosecutes misdemeanor crimes in the county courts. The county attorney also advises the county commissioners and other county officials about legal matters.

county court: the trial court that hears most misdemeanor cases and appeals from criminal cases in justice and municipal courts. The judge of this court also is the chief executive of the county government.

county court at law: the court created by the legislature in most of the larger counties to hear most misdemeanor cases and appeals from criminal cases from justice and municipal courts. A county court at law judge does not have the administrative duties that a county judge has.

court: the institution created by a governing body and given the power to try criminal cases.

court administrator: the officer who schedules cases for the court.

court-appointed lawyer: the lawyer assigned by a judge to defend indigent defendants. This lawyer is paid by the local county an amount that is usually less than the normal fee. If the defendants are convicted, the judge can order that they pay this money back to the local county.

court of appeals: the court that reviews criminal convictions to determine whether the defendant received a fair trial. Each of these 14 courts serves a different geographical area of the state.

Court of Criminal Appeals: the highest court in Texas that can review a criminal case. Appeals of death penalty cases go directly to the Court of Criminal Appeals. The court also may decide to review decisions of the court of appeals. The Court of Criminal Appeals meets in Austin and has nine judges, each of whom is elected on a statewide basis.

court reporter: the person who is responsible for writing down every word spoken in the courtroom.

court residential treatment facility (CRTF): the residential facility designed to house probationers. CRTFs provide a number of general rehabilitation programs.

crime victim: the person who is directly affected or injured by the criminal conduct of another. Most laws giving rights to crime victims limit "crime victim" to victims of only violent crimes. See also *victim*.

Crime Victims' Bill of Rights: the portion of the state constitution that guarantees certain rights to crime victims.

Crime Victims' Compensation Act: the law that allows victims of violent crimes to receive reimbursement for financial losses that are not reimbursed from other sources.

crime victim liaison (CVL): the employee of each local law enforcement agency who is responsible for ensuring that all victims receive the information and services that the law guarantees them.

criminal law: the group of laws that defines crimes and sets their punishment. The Texas Legislature makes the criminal laws of Texas.

cross-examination: the process of questioning the witness by the lawyer who did not call the witness to testify. Cross-examination occurs after direct examination.

culpable mental state: the legal requirement that defendants must have voluntarily committed crime by intending it, by knowing that they were committing it, or by acting in a negligent or reckless manner. See also *intentional, knowing, negligent*, and *reckless.*

custody: the term for juvenile arrest.

D.A.R.E. (Drug Abuse Resistance Education): nationwide drug education program taught by uniformed law enforcement officers in conjunction with a classroom teacher.

death penalty: the execution of a convicted murderer by the state. In Texas, the death penalty is administered by a lethal injection of poison.

defendant: the person formally accused of a crime.

defense lawyer: the lawyer who represents defendants in criminal cases. It is his or her job, within certain ethical rules, to prevent defendants from being convicted and, if they are convicted, to obtain the lightest possible punishment. See also *prosecutor.*

deferred adjudication: the probation for which the judge hears evidence of the defendants' guilt but does not actually convict them of crimes. Conditions of a deferred adjudication are the same as those of a regular probation. See also *probation.*

delinquent conduct: the broad category of serious juvenile misconduct. All felonies and most serious misdemeanors are examples of delinquent conduct. See also *conduct indicating a need for supervision.*

detention hearing: the proceeding in court to determine whether a juvenile in custody should continue to be detained or should be released to a parent or other appropriate person. See also *hearing.*

determinate sentencing: the proceeding which allows juveniles to be tried in the juvenile system but to receive fixed sentences that can include confinement in a Texas Youth Commission facility with a possible transfer to the adult prison system at age 18.

direct examination: the process of questioning a witness by the lawyer, either the prosecutor or defense lawyer, who called the witness to testify. Direct examination occurs before cross-examination.

disposition hearing: the proceeding in court to determine a juvenile's sentence. This hearing is the juvenile system's equivalent of the punishment phase of an adult trial. Unlike adults, juveniles generally have no right to a jury at a disposition hearing. See also *hearing*.

district attorney: the elected local official who prosecutes felony crimes in the district courts of the geographical area he or she represents.

district court: the principal trial court in Texas. District courts hear all felony cases and misdemeanor cases involving official corruption.

DNA (deoxyribonucleic acid): the material located in all living cells. DNA forms a unique "blueprint" for that organism. Scientists compare DNA in living cells (such as blood, hair, or semen) left at a crime scene with a suspect's DNA to help identify the person who committed the crime.

docket: the list of cases that a court will hear on a given day or week.

docket call: the calling of all the cases set to be heard by the judge at a certain time. Docket calls often are used to determine whether defendants have lawyers and whether they want to plead guilty or have a trial.

drug-free zone: the area within 1,000 feet of a school or playground or within 300 feet of a youth center, public pool, or video arcade. Drug offenses committed within these zones carry increased minimum punishments and tough parole rules.

drug testing: the urine test to determine whether an individual has recently used drugs or alcohol. Drug testing is often used as a condition for pretrial release, probation, or parole.

early termination: the conclusion of a probation, for good behavior, before the entire term has been completed.

electronic monitoring: the automated system that determines whether or not individuals leave their homes. This system is used to monitor defendants ordered to remain at home during certain times or for certain periods. Electronic monitoring is sometimes used as a condition of pretrial release, probation, or parole.

enhancement: the use of a prior conviction to increase the punishment range on a new conviction.

entrapment: the illegal inducement by a law enforcement officer that causes someone to commit a crime that he or she was not predisposed to commit.

evidence: all of the testimony and physical items which can be considered by the judge or jury in deciding a case.

examining trial: the hearing that requires the prosecutor to call witnesses to establish probable cause for the judge to believe that the defendants committed the crimes the prosecutor charges them with committing. An indictment eliminates defendants' rights to an examining trial.

excited utterance: the hearsay statement made while a person is under the immediate influence of an excited or startling event, such as a crime. These statements (such as a 911 tape) are allowed into evidence even though they are hearsay.

exhibit: any piece of evidence that is brought into the courtroom and marked for identification.

expert witness: the witness who has the education or experience that allows him or her to interpret evidence for a jury. Unlike other witnesses, expert witnesses can give their opinions about the evidence. Physicians and chemists are examples of frequently used expert witnesses.

extradition: the process of bringing defendants from the state where they were arrested to the state where they are charged with crimes.

felony: a more serious crime than the misdemeanor. This crime has a maximum possible punishment of confinement in a state jail or state prison or the death penalty. See also *misdemeanor*.

fine: the form of criminal punishment that requires defendants to pay a certain cash amount. Fines go to the general fund of the governing body of the court.

fingerprint: the impression left on an object when it is touched by a finger. The impression shows the ridges in the skin. The pattern of these ridges is different in every person.

foreperson: the man or woman who leads the trial jury or grand jury in its decision-making process. Grand jury forepersons are selected by the district judge; trial jury forepersons are selected by the jury members.

furlough: the temporary leave of absence granted to prison inmates.

good time: the extra time credits given to nonviolent offenders. It can allow them to become eligible for parole or release after serving a small fraction of their sentences.

grand jury: the group of 12 citizens who must determine whether there is enough evidence to bring criminal charges against the accused. Grand jurors meet for a specific period of time, usually two to six months. All felony defendants in Texas must be indicted by a grand jury unless they specifically give up this right.

grand jury commission: the group of three to five citizens selected by a district judge for the purpose of selecting a grand jury. The commissioners select up to 40 citizens who are notified to appear before the district judge. The first 12 who are qualified to serve then become the grand jury.

guilt phase: the first part of a criminal trial during which the jury determines whether or not the defendant is guilty as charged. See also *punishment phase*.

guilty plea: a plea option along with not guilty and nolo contendere. Defendants admit that the charges against them are true. Such a plea waives their rights to have the state prove the charges. Before accepting guilty pleas, a judge must be satisfied that the defendants' pleas are both voluntary and knowing. The judge normally questions the defendants before accepting guilty pleas. See also *not guilty* and *nolo contendere*.

habeas corpus: the legal challenge to a conviction that can be brought after the trial and all appeals are over. There is no time limit for filing a habeas corpus. The term also applies to a motion to reduce the amount of bail before the trial.

habitual criminal: the defendant who has two or more separate prior prison sentences.

hate crime: the crime whose victim is selected because of the defendant's bias or prejudice against the victim or the ethnic, religious, sexual, or gender group to which the victim belongs.

hearing: the court proceeding for the judge to hear evidence and arguments from the lawyers. In common usage, a hearing is any such proceeding except the actual trial that decides whether the defendants are guilty or not guilty.

hearsay: the statement made outside of court that was heard by a witness. Hearsay is not allowed in a courtroom unless it is one of the exceptions to the hearsay rule. For example, statements by defendants and by victims made immediately after an exciting or startling event (such as the crime) are allowed to be used as evidence.

homicide: the unlawful taking of another person's life. This general term includes capital murder, intentional murder, manslaughter, intoxication manslaughter, and criminally negligent homicide. See also *capital murder, culpable mental state, manslaughter*, and *murder*.

hung jury: the jury unable to reach a unanimous verdict even though the jurors have made every effort to discuss the evidence and arrive at a unanimous verdict.

indictment: the written document that contains the legal charges against defendants. An indictment can be issued only by a grand jury after it has found enough evidence to believe that the crime was probably committed by the defendants. Indictments are required in all felony cases; they are occasionally used in misdemeanor cases. See also *information*.

indigent: the defendant who is too poor to pay for a lawyer. Indigent defendants are provided lawyers by the judge who hears their case.

individual voir dire: the process of questioning potential jurors one at a time outside the presence of the other potential jurors. Individual voir dire is used in all cases where the prosecutor is seeking the death penalty. See also *voir dire.*

information: the written document that contains legal charges against defendants. Informations are signed by a prosecutor and do not involve a grand jury. Informations are used for most misdemeanor offenses and for felonies when the defendants give up their right to a grand jury indictment. See also *indictment.*

insanity: a legal defense to criminal charges. Defendants must prove that, at the time of the crime, they had a severe mental disease or defect that caused them not to know that the action was a crime. Insanity is very seldom used successfully in Texas.

Institutional Division: the official name for the Texas state prison system. See also *Texas Department of Criminal Justice.*

intentional: the state of mind required for some crimes. The state must prove that defendants desired to commit the crimes. See also *culpable mental state.*

intermediate sanction facility: the secure facility, similar to a county jail, where probationers can be confined for up to six months instead of having their probations revoked.

intoxication: the loss of normal mental or physical abilities caused by alcohol or drugs.

investigation: the process of determining the facts related to a crime, including who committed the crime.

Jackson v Denno hearing: the proceeding in court usually before the actual trial to determine whether any confessions made by defendants were voluntary. If the confessions were not voluntary, the judge will rule that they may not be used during the trial. The hearing gets its name from the U.S. Supreme Court case that requires such a hearing. See also *hearing.*

jail: the county-run facility designed both to hold defendants awaiting trial and to incarcerate defendants convicted of misdemeanors. See also *state jail.*

judge: the official who presides over a courtroom. The judge determines what the law is and how it applies to a case. If there is no jury, the judge also determines the facts of the case.

juror: a member of a jury.

jury: the group of citizens who must determine whether a defendant is guilty or not guilty. The jury also sets the punishment if the defendant so requests. A felony jury has 12 members and a misdemeanor jury has 6 members. Jury decisions in Texas criminal cases must be made by a unanimous vote.

jury charge: the judge's written instruction to the jury. It explains the law that applies to the case, the facts the jury is to decide, and the general instructions about how the jury is to work.

jury trial: the trial at which juries determine whether or not the defendants are guilty. Prosecutors and defendants have a right to a jury trial on the issue of guilt. Defendants have the option of either the judge or the same jury determining their sentences.

justice court: the court created by the legislature to hear traffic and other minor criminal cases that arise from actions that occur in areas outside of cities served by municipal courts.

juvenile: a child who is at least 10 years old but not yet 17. Children in this age range when they commit certain improper conduct are subject to the juvenile system.

juvenile board: the local board composed of judges who oversee the juvenile probation department and designate the juvenile court. Each county is served by a juvenile board.

juvenile court: the local court or courts designated by the juvenile board to hear juvenile cases. The juvenile court must be either a district or a county court.

Juvenile Probation Department: the local agency that processes juvenile cases and supervises juveniles placed on probation.

knowing: a state of mind required for some crimes. The state must prove that defendants were aware that they were committing the crimes. See also *culpable mental state*.

law enforcement officer: the person licensed by the State of Texas to enforce laws. Law enforcement officers must be employed by a law enforcement agency, take a 560-hour training course, and pass a written examination. Licenses are issued by the Texas Commission on Law Enforcement Officer Standards and Education.

magistrate: the term for any judge performing administrative duties such as signing search warrants, setting bail, or warning defendants of their legal rights.

mandate: the final written order of an appellate court ordering that a conviction be upheld, a new trial be granted, or a finding of not guilty be entered.

mandatory supervision: the automatic release from prison of non-violent offenders when the total calendar time plus all good-time credits equals the total sentence.

manslaughter: the unintentional but reckless taking of another person's life. See also *homicide*.

Miranda warnings: the information about legal rights to remain silent and to have a lawyer. After an arrest, law enforcement officers must tell suspects about these rights before asking questions. The name comes from the criminal defendant, Ernesto Miranda, in the 1966 U.S. Supreme Court case that required these warnings be given.

misdemeanor: a less serious crime than the felony. This crime has a maximum possible punishment of either confinement in a local county jail or simply a fine. See also *felony.*

mistrial: the declaration by the judge ending the trial because something happened that made a fair trial impossible or because of a hung jury. Normally, a case can be tried again when the first trial results in a mistrial.

motion to revoke: the legal document filed by the prosecutor setting out violations of a probation and asking the judge to revoke the probation.

motion to suppress: the legal document filed by the defense lawyer before trial. The motion sets out some legal reason, usually police misconduct, why some or all of the evidence against the defendant should not be allowed to be used at the trial.

municipal court: the court created by a city government to hear traffic and other minor criminal cases which occur within the city. See also *justice court.*

murder: the intentional, unlawful taking of another person's life. See also *homicide.*

National DNA Index System (NDIS): national database that links statewide databases into a nationwide system for matching unknown DNA with known offenders. Cf. *Automated Fingerprint Identification System (AFIS); Combined DNA Index System (CODIS).*

National Integrated Ballistics Information Network (NIBIN): national database that allows ballistic evidence to be matched in an attempt to link shooting incidents. Cf. *Automated Fingerprint Identification System (AFIS); Combined DNA Index System (CODIS).*

negligent (or criminally negligent): a required state of mind for some crimes. The state must prove that defendants should have been aware that their actions could have dangerous consequences. See also *culpable mental state.*

no-bill: the action of a grand jury that votes not to indict a defendant. At least four votes are required to no-bill a defendant. This action serves to dismiss a case and end any criminal prosecution. See also *true bill.*

nolo contendere: a plea option, along with guilty and not guilty. Defendants do not contest the charges and understand that they will be found guilty without a trial or a guilty plea. See also *guilty* and *not guilty.*

not-guilty plea: a plea option, along with guilty and nolo contendere. Defendants contest the charges and challenge the state to prove them beyond a reasonable doubt. In capital murder cases, a not-guilty plea is mandatory. See also *guilty* and *nolo contendere.*

notice of appeal: the legal document filed by the defense lawyers informing the trial court that they want an appellate court to review a conviction.

objection: the legal argument in the courtroom against allowing a question to be asked or another event to occur. Either the prosecutor or the defense lawyer may object. The judge must either overrule or sustain. See also *overruled* and *sustained.*

opening statement: the oral summary of the evidence made by the prosecutor or defense lawyer at the beginning of a trial. See also *closing statement.*

oral argument: the appearance by the defense lawyer and the prosecutor before an appellate court. Both sides explain their briefs and answer any questions from the judges. No new evidence can be considered at this time.

overruled: the judge's ruling on an objection by the defense lawyer or the prosecutor. The judge disagrees with the objection and allows the continuation of whatever is being objected to. See also *sustained.*

Pardons and Paroles Division: the part of the Texas Department of Criminal Justice that supervises parolees (similar to the Community Supervision and Corrections Department, which supervises probationers). See also *Texas Department of Criminal Justice.*

parole: the supervised release of convicted defendants after they have served a portion of their sentences in prison. Parole release is subject to conditions set by the parole board. Violation of these conditions can result in arrest and a return to prison. See also *probation.*

parole board: the 18-member board that decides whether to grant, deny, or revoke paroles.

parole in absentia: the practice of paroling inmates directly from a county jail even though they were sentenced to prison.

parole officer: the individual who monitors defendants on parole.

parole protest: the request to the parole board to deny a parole.

peace officer: another term for law enforcement officer.

penal code: the collection of the major crimes and their punishments. These laws are passed by the Texas Legislature.

penalty paragraph: the part of an indictment that details prior prison sentences. If the prosecution proves this paragraph at the punishment phase, the possible sentence is increased.

peremptory challenges: the right of both the prosecutor and the defense lawyer to eliminate a potential juror without stating a reason. Both sides have an equal number of such challenges, ranging from three in a misdemeanor trial to 15 in a death penalty trial.

personal bond: the bond that pledges no cash or other security. The judge may impose conditions on this type of release. In some counties, defendants released on personal bonds are supervised much as defendants on probation. These defendants can be charged a small fee for release. See also *bond*.

petition for discretionary review: the written request from either the prosecution or defense lawyer for the Court of Criminal Appeals to change a ruling made by the court of appeals. The Court of Criminal Appeals grants very few of these requests.

plea: the defendants' formal response to the charges against them. They can enter a plea of guilty, nolo contendere, or not guilty. If defendants refuse to enter a plea, the judge enters a not-guilty plea for them. See also *guilty, nolo contendere*, and *not guilty*.

plea bargaining: the process that lets the prosecutor and defense lawyer negotiate the outcome of criminal cases. The bargain includes what charges defendants will be convicted of and what sentences they will serve. In Texas, plea bargaining agreements must be in writing. The judge may either accept or reject the agreement.

predicate: the facts which must be proved before the judge can allow an exhibit to become part of the evidence in a case.

pre-parole transfer: the practice of transferring inmates from prison to a less secure facility a few months before they become eligible for parole.

preponderance of the evidence: the legal requirement that evidence show a fact more likely than not is true. Defendants must prove insanity by a preponderance of the evidence. See also *beyond a reasonable doubt*.

pre-sentence report: the written document filed by a probation officer. The report provides background information about defendants, their crimes, and the impact on any victims. The judge uses this information for sentencing.

presumption of innocence: the legal presumption that all defendants are innocent until they are proven guilty.

pretrial hearing: the proceeding in court before the actual trial. At this hearing, the judge listens to evidence and arguments from prosecutors and defense lawyers about legal issues affecting the trial. See also *hearing*.

privilege: the right of an individual not to testify about certain matters. For example, defendants have the privilege not to have their lawyers testify about things the defendants have told them.

probable cause: the reasonable belief based upon all of the facts that some event or conclusion is true. For example, law enforcement officers need probable cause to obtain search warrants and arrest warrants.

probation: the supervised release of convicted defendants after a judge has suspended their sentences. Probation is subject to conditions imposed by the judge. Violation of these conditions subjects the defendant to arrest and prison. Probation is officially known in Texas as community supervision. See also *parole.*

probation condition: the specific behavior a probationer must abide by or be subject to having probation revoked. This condition is imposed by the sentencing judge.

probation officer: the individual who monitors defendants on probation.

promiscuity defense: the legal defense that excused defendants of statutory rape of 14-, 15- and 16-year-old victims if the victims had some prior sexual activity. For crimes occurring after August 31, 1994, the legislature abolished this defense.

prosecutor: the lawyer who represents the state in criminal cases. It is his or her job, within certain ethical rules, to convict defendants and, if they are convicted, to obtain the severest possible punishment. Prosecutors may be district attorneys, county attorneys, or city attorneys, depending on the court where they prosecute cases.

protective order: the order from a judge designed to make an individual do something or stop doing something. These orders protect victims from future acts of family violence.

punishment phase: the second part of a criminal trial during which the jury, having already found the defendant guilty, determines the sentence. Evidence of other convictions and bad acts of the defendant can be introduced at the punishment phase; such evidence is not allowed at the guilt phase. See also *guilt phase.*

rape crisis center: the victim support agency that provides direct services to victims of sexual assault.

reasonable doubt. See *beyond a reasonable doubt.*

rebuttal: the evidence offered by either the prosecutor or defense lawyer to contradict evidence offered by the other side.

reckless: a state of mind required for some crimes. The state must prove that defendants were aware that their actions could have dangerous consequences but chose to ignore the risk. See also *culpable mental state.*

record: the official recording of the trial as it is preserved by the court reporter. The record includes everything that is said at trial along with all of the exhibits.

relevant: the standard of whether or not a piece of evidence makes a fact either more likely or less likely to be true.

restitution: the payment by defendants to victims or government agencies of costs associated with a crime, investigation, or prosecution.

restitution center: the nonsecure residential facility where probationers are required to work at an outside job and use their wages to pay room and board, support their dependents, and make financial restitution to their victims.

reverse: the ruling of an appeals court that grants a new trial or enters a not-guilty verdict.

revocation: the act of the sentencing judge or parole board in ending a probation or parole because of a violation of one or more conditions. For probation, the judge then sentences the probationer to a period of confinement. For parole, the board then returns the parolee to prison.

right not to testify: the right of criminal defendants not to testify or even be called as witnesses in their own trials. The jury is instructed that the fact that a defendant has not testified is not to be considered as any evidence of guilt.

rule of evidence: the written rule that tells a judge whether or not to allow testimony or physical items as evidence in a case. The rules are written by the Court of Criminal Appeals.

rule of witnesses: the rule that allows either the prosecutor or the defense lawyer to exclude from the courtroom all witnesses except when they are testifying. This rule does not apply to defendants, but it does apply to victims.

search: the process of a peace officer looking for contraband or other evidence of a crime.

search warrant: the written document from a magistrate authorizing a law enforcement officer to search a particular thing or place for specified pieces of contraband or evidence.

self-defense: a legal defense for the use of force to prevent harm from another person.

serve all: the action of the parole board of denying parole and requiring inmates to serve their entire sentences without further review.

sheriff: the elected county official who operates the county jail and provides primary law enforcement services for unincorporated areas of a county.

shock probation: the sentence that first incarcerates defendants for up to 180 days and then begins their probation.

stalking: the form of harassment in which a person repeatedly follows or otherwise contacts a victim to annoy or threaten.

state jail: the minimum security state prison; it has more rehabilitation programs available than conventional prisons. See also *jail.*

state jail felony: the lowest level of felony. It is punishable by a sentence of six months to two years in a state jail. The judge may also impose a fine of up to $10,000.

statement of facts: the verbatim text of every word spoken at trial by the lawyers, witnesses, and judge. This text is prepared by the court reporter and is forwarded to the appellate court when a case is appealed. See also *transcript.*

subpoena: the written order requiring a witness to appear in court on a certain day at a certain time.

subpoena duces tecum: the written order requiring a witness to appear in court and bring specified documents or other items.

substance abuse felony punishment facility: the secure prison-type facility designed to provide intensive in-patient drug treatment for probationers.

substance abuse treatment facility (SATF): the residential facility designed to house probationers. SATFs specialize in providing drug treatment programs along with a number of general rehabilitation programs.

surety bond: the bond that pledges a refundable dollar payment if the defendant makes all court appearances. Most surety bonds are written by bail bonding companies that require defendants to pay a nonrefundable fee of 10% to 20% of the dollar amount. See also *bond.*

sustained: the judge's ruling on an objection. He or she agrees with the objection and will not allow the continuation of whatever is being objected to. See also *overruled.*

termination: the conclusion of a probation that has not been revoked.

testify: the act of being a witness in court and answering questions from the lawyers. See also *witness.*

Texas Crime Victim Clearinghouse: the part of the Texas Department of Criminal Justice that provides victims with information and referrals. The office also trains various groups on victim-related topics.

Texas Department of Criminal Justice: the agency that controls the entire state correctional program, including probation, prison, and parole. See also *Community Supervision and Corrections Department, Institutional Division,* and *Pardons and Paroles Division.*

Texas Juvenile Probation Commission (TJPC): the agency that has general oversight responsibilities for local juvenile probation departments. The TJPC channels state funding to those departments.

Texas Youth Commission (TYC): the agency responsible for the juvenile corrections system.

transcript: the clerk's official collection of all written motions and all written orders issued by the judge. The transcript is prepared and forwarded to the appellate court when a case is appealed. See also *statement of facts*.

trial: the proceeding in court that determines the guilt and punishment of defendants.

trial court: the courts where trials of accused defendants are held. For defendants found guilty, the trial court also sets punishment.

trial de novo: the appeal from justice court and most municipal courts conducted as an entirely new trial in a county court.

true bill: the action of a grand jury that votes to indict a defendant. At least nine votes are required to "true bill" a defendant. After voting a true bill, an indictment is prepared and signed by the grand jury foreperson. See also *no-bill*.

unanimous verdict: the legal requirement in a Texas criminal case. All members of a jury must agree with the decision about guilt and the sentence.

venire: the group of potential jurors from which a jury is picked.

venue: the county in which a case may be prosecuted. In most criminal cases, the case must be prosecuted in the county where the crime occurred.

verdict: the decision of a jury.

victim: the person who is harmed by a crime. See also *crime victim*.

victim assistance coordinator (VAC): the employee of each district and county attorney's office who is responsible for ensuring that crime victims receive all the services that the law guarantees them.

Victim Assistance Resource Directory: the book published by the Crime Victim Clearinghouse that lists hundreds of resources available for crime victims and professionals.

victim impact statement: the written form a victim may use to explain to the judge the effects, financial and otherwise, of a crime. Prosecutors provide these forms to victims of violent crimes. The prosecutor gives the completed form to the judge before sentencing.

voir dire: the process of jury selection. Both the prosecutor and defense lawyer question a group of potential jurors. See also *individual voir dire*.

waiver: the act of giving up a legal right. If defendants waive legal rights, they must do so knowingly and intelligently. They must understand the right and the consequences of giving it up.

witness: the person who, after being sworn to tell the truth, tells about facts of the case in response to the prosecutor's and defense lawyer's questions. See also *testify*.

work release: the sentence that confines defendants to jail but releases them each day to go to work.

Wyndham school district: the in-prison school district run exclusively for inmates by the Texas Department of Criminal Justice. Its programs roughly parallel the courses, both academic and vocational, of the public school system.

INDEX

(The Appendix lists the sections of the Penal Code that apply to individual crimes and their punishment ranges.)